# THE  BEATITUDES

Other books by Bernard Häring CSsR
published by St Paul Publications

    Evangelization today
    Faith and morality in a secular age
    Sin in the secular age
    The sacraments in a secular age
    Hope is the remedy
    Prayer: the integration of faith and life
    Medical Ethics
    Manipulation

Bernard Häring

# THE BEATITUDES

**Their personal and
social implications**

 St Paul Publications

ST PAUL PUBLICATIONS
SLOUGH   SL3 6BT   ENGLAND

Copyright © Bernard Häring 1976

Nihil obstat: D. Valente
Imprimatur:  + Charles Grant, Bishop of Northampton
             19 July 1976

First Published October 1976

Printed in Great Britain by the Society of St. Paul, Slough

ISBN 0 85439 130 4

# CONTENTS

## ACKNOWLEDGEMENTS

I wish to thank all who, with me, have meditated on and tried to live the beatitudes.

I thank Sister Constance Guilbeault, S.C.O., for patiently transcribing the tapes.

I sincerely thank Sister Gabrielle L. Jean for her interest and her care in editing the text.

B.H.

May, 1976

# Chapter 1

# THE JOY OF THE LORD IS OUR STRENGTH

Christianity becomes a promise and a source of salvation for the world whenever people share the belief of St Francis and his brothers: 'We can live the gospel: we want to live it and, of course, we must live it'. The joy of faith is at the very heart of Christianity. Faith is essentially a glad and grateful acceptance of the saving truth and entails a total commitment to it.

It may be that today we understand better than earlier generations the words of St James: 'You have faith enough to believe that there is one God. Excellent! The devils have faith like that, and it makes them tremble' (James 2:19-20).

Faith or orthodoxy without joy is not only unattractive but it is also incapable of producing a genuine Christian life. The joy of the Lord is the very strength that transforms us into witnesses and servants of our brothers and sisters. Thus, the gospel proclaimed by our Lord Jesus Christ tells us that we are living in a favoured time, that God guides us by his own love and unites us in his presence. And from there, then, arises the moral imperative as good news: 'The time has come; the kingdom of God is upon you; be renewed in your mind and believe in the gospel' (Mk 1:15). In the context, it is evident that Jesus is reminding us of the prophecies, namely, that God will gather us, give us a new heart, a new spirit, and that we can live in this spirit. But the transforming power through which God's grace becomes operative is the joyful trust that we are capable of living the gospel.

The Second Vatican Council emphasized that all people are called to holiness of life. No one holds a monopoly of holiness, but anyone who manifests the joy of the gospel in his whole life witnesses to this universal vocation. There are some people who have received the particular charism of faith whereby they can communicate to others, together with the joy of faith, the conviction that everybody can live the gospel of purity of heart, of gentleness, of non-violence, of total commitment to the good of their brothers and sisters.

Today, one no longer considers a priestly or a religious vocation as creating a ritual orientation or a privileged class. Contemporary men and women look for persons who are totally dedicated to the gospel, that is, who live it and help others come to the same joy and thus discover the strength to set out in the direction of the gospel. I consider prayer and meditation as expressions of this joy, as a longing to receive it and to be able to share it with others. Whenever this happens, people are truly gathered in the name of Jesus. It is then that each family, a community of priests, brothers or sisters, live and pray together. Authentic religious communities and prayer groups give us an idea of how the promise of the prophets will be fulfilled: 'I will bring them to my holy mountain and give them joy in my house of prayer. Their offerings and sacrifices shall be accepted on my altar; for my house shall be called a house of prayer for all nations' (Isaiah 56:7).

The following meditations are based on the conviction that Christian life is essentially a manifestation of the beatitudes, and that all the disciples of Christ can find guidance for a life of faith and graciousness in the sermon on the mount. The great Mahatma Gandhi meditated on the beatitudes with his friends in his ashrams, his houses of prayer, and they found there the energies for their non-violent efforts for liberation. We should all come together frequently, open ourselves to the joy of the beatitudes, and meditate on how we can live them in the conditions of life in today's world.

'When he saw the crowds he went up the hill. There he took his seat, and when his disciples had gathered around him, he began to address them' (Mt 5:1-2). Close attention should be

2

given to each word of the introduction since it provides the key to our understanding of the whole sermon on the mount.

One could think that Jesus tried to escape the crowd by going up the mount where his disciples gathered around him, but this would contradict the whole of the gospel and of our faith. Jesus loves the crowd; he came as the Saviour of the world; he shed his blood on Mount Calvary for all men. When Jesus gathers his disciples around him, his heart goes out to all men even if he attends more specially to those who follow him up the hill to the mount of the beatitudes.

We cannot truly find Christ and dwell with him unless we join him in his love of all people. But for us to join Christ in his love of people we must really gather around him and come to know him intimately as the Emmanuel, God with us. Whoever conceives the main purpose of life to be keeping busy with others will never radiate the joy, goodness, gentleness and mercy of the Lord. If we wish to make Christ known to all people, we must first know him and know him as his friends did — as listeners, as persons ready to follow him, even if the way sometimes seems arduous.

We can never allow ourselves as Christians to flee from people, but we are allowed and even urged to retreat from the noise, the distractions and the idols of the marketplace. Then, once we have found Christ and have listened to him, once we have come to know him in his infinite love and compassion for all people, he can send us saying: 'You are the light of the world'.

We can never learn the wonderful gospel of the beatitudes by means of scientific study. In no way do I want to minimize theological research and reflection, but at the very heart of theology and Christian faith is the experience of Christ's nearness. He came from heaven for our salvation and for the redemption of all mankind.

Jesus tells us: 'I am the vine; you are the branches. He who dwells in me bears much fruit; for apart from me you can do nothing' (Jn 15:5). The Lord loses no time in informing us of the harvest of our abiding with him: 'This is my Father's glory, that you may bear fruit in plenty and so be my disciples'

(Jn 15:8). Christ proclaims the beatitudes and shares with us the knowledge of the Father so that our heart may be filled with joy. If we truly abide in his love and rejoice in his nearness, treasuring up his words in our heart and mind, then we shall come to know his love for all people; we too can then become a source of joy for many people. But because of our selfishness, we have to remind ourselves, from time to time, that we cannot be with Christ and rejoice in him unless we turn our eyes to the multitude as he did when he went up the mount of the beatitudes.

In each of the following meditations on the beatitudes, we shall take three steps, each one interlocking with the others.

(1) We shall first allow ourselves full awareness of Christ's presence and remind ourselves that he is the beatitude incarnate and that we cannot understand the height and depth, the beauty of his message in the beatitudes unless we know and recognize him as the source of all joy and all goodness.

(2) We shall then meditate on Christ's personal calling to live with him the gospel of the beatitudes.

(3) Then we can give special attention to the social implications of each of the beatitudes in order to understand better our mission to be the light of the world and the salt of the earth.

\* \* \*

Lord Jesus Christ, I thank you for having revealed yourself to us as the Emmanuel, as God with us. There is no greater joy in this world than to dwell with you, to rejoice in your friendship. You have called me with so many others to join you on the path leading to the mount of the beatitudes, to proclaim the same message of joy as you did two thousand years ago to James, John, Peter and your other disciples. You want to share with us your love of the Father and your love of all people, as well as your joy; you shared these treasures with your disciples who listened to your words when you walked with them through Galilee and Judea.

4

Lord, I will always reserve time to become aware of your nearness, to treasure up your words, but make me equally conscious of the fact that I cannot stay with you and rejoice in your friendship unless I am as concerned for the multitude as you were. For you grant me the privilege of dwelling with you not so much for me to think of myself; it is given to me with a view to a mission. Help us all to come to the understanding that we cannot be of help to the world unless we dwell with you, and that we cannot dwell with you, rejoice in you, unless we accept our mission to be a living gospel for our fellowmen.

Lord, here I am; call me.
Lord, here I am; send me.

Chapter 2

# BLESSED ARE THOSE WHO KNOW THEIR NEED OF GOD; THE KINGDOM OF GOD IS THEIRS

## 1. *Christ, the Servant*

Before us stands Christ, the Son of God and the son of man, who made himself the servant of all; he identifies himself with the humble ones for he has come to bear their burdens. He who made himself the most lowly in his human life is the greatest in the kingdom of God. He made himself poor in order to enrich us all, and so he can rejoice in the Holy Spirit: 'I thank you, Father, Lord of heaven and earth, for hiding these things from the learned and wise, and revealing them to the simple. Yes, Father, such was your choice. Everything is entrusted to me by my Father; and no one knows who the Son is but the Father, or who the Father is but the Son, and those to whom the Son may choose to reveal him' (Lk 10:21-22). After this exultant prayer, Jesus turned to his disciples and said: 'Happy the eyes that see what you are seeing' (Lk 10:23).

Happy are we if we recognize Jesus as the Servant and are ready to follow him, to be with him in his service to the brethren. Christ is anointed by the Holy Spirit for his ministry. He is filled with the joy of the Father in the Holy Spirit so that he can make himself one of the most lowly in the country. Jesus grew up with Mary and Joseph, who wonderfully represented the humble and lowly people, the *anawim* of the country, who expected the coming of the Messiah with a view to freeing the oppressed. Jesus saw how these *anawim* understood the secrets of the kingdom of God and he looked forward to all those saints who, like St Francis, had chosen simplicity and poverty as their brides.

It is important to look to the Exemplar before asking abstract questions about poverty. We are faced with Jesus' whole life and even more so with his death, which speak of him who, by the power of the Holy Spirit, made himself a poor servant of all men. When Jesus first spoke publicly in the synagogue of his home, Nazareth, he read the great canticle of the servant of Yahweh as it is written by the second Isaiah: 'The Spirit of the Lord is upon me because he has anointed me; he has sent me to announce good news to the poor, to proclaim release for prisoners and recovery of sight for the blind; to let the broken victims go free, to proclaim the year of the Lord's favour'. And then Jesus made known his identity to his hearers: 'Today', he said, 'in your very hearing, this text has come true' (Lk 4: 18-21).

In accordance with the will of the Father, Jesus chose not only a life among the poor but a life totally dedicated to all the lowly, the poor, the suffering, the sinners. He could do so with joy because he was filled with the Holy Spirit. In his poverty, as in his service, he opens our eyes and our heart to the richness of a life in the service of God and our fellowmen. Jesus finds his joy in healing the sick, in freeing the oppressed, in proclaiming the good news to the poor.

Jesus manifests the meaning of his state of poverty and of service to the poor when he insists that he did not come to seek his own glory and to do his own will but to seek the glory of the Father. He unmasks the lust for power and reveals the kingdom of the Father by his humble service. He shares more specially in the kingdom of the Father in that he reveals this kingdom through his total dedication to the service of all people. Therefore, the Father exalted him and gave him a name above all names. He is called Lord, and this in view of his free choice to be the servant of all, especially the servant of the poor and

8

of the oppressed. If Christ had not made himself a humble servant, then there would have been no possibility of proclaiming the beatitude: 'Blessed are those who, by the Spirit, know that they are in need of God. The kingdom of God is theirs'.

Jesus not only turns his eyes and his heart to the multitude but he presents himself, in all his life, as the One consecrated to the service of this worried multitude. It is for this mission that he was anointed by the Holy Spirit.

The Church continues the event of Pentecost whenever she identifies with Mary, the humble handmaid, and thus follows Christ, the Servant. Only through the power of the Holy Spirit can we come to understand the depth and the height, the breadth and the length of this beatitude personified in Christ, the Servant, whom the Father proclaimed Lord. The Holy Spirit renews and vivifies the spirit of the disciples of Christ so that they can treasure up the gospel in their hearts, experience the joy of the good news, and rejoicingly declare: 'We can live the gospel; we want to live it'. By the power of the Holy Spirit, Christ has freed us from the collective slavery of sinfulness that manifests itself in the lust for power, in exploitation, in contempt for the poor and the weak. By making himself a servant and doing so with joy, Christ paved for us the path to freedom and joy.

They alone can come to the knowledge of Christ who are ready to follow Christ on to the mount of the beatitudes where he proclaims the mission of the servant. 'For you know how generous our Lord Jesus Christ has been; he was rich; yet for your sake he became poor, so that through his poverty you might become rich' (2 Cor 8:9). This enthusiastic appeal of the apostle Paul tells us that Christ did not come to build up a welfare society; even less did he want to build a society wherein a few would constitute a privileged class. However, Paul shows us that we can make good use of material goods, the gifts of God, in order to form a brotherly society in which all rejoice in the gifts and the blessings of the One God and Father, and the One Lord, Jesus Christ.

He who follows Christ onto the mount of the beatitudes in the readiness to know him as servant experiences a radical

9

liberation from the lust to possess, to dominate others or to manipulate his fellowman. Those who honour the weak, the powerless, the simple, come to a realization of their own dignity as free human persons.

There is a singular joy in sharing with others. Christ knows perfectly that all that he is, and has, is a gift from the Father. This gift from the Father he received with joy and gratitude; he realizes that he is the Father's incarnate Son for the sake of the multitude. Therefore, his readiness to be the servant of all is only a part and a privileged expression of his joy and gratitude towards the Father.

\* \* \*

Lord Jesus Christ, you have made known the kingdom of the Father as a servant. So often when we speak of God's glory and of his kingdom we blur the message because we place ourselves at the very centre, or, to say the least, confuse people by our mixed motives. You have come to be the servant and you have taught us how to serve, that is, how to share in the kingdom of the Father. Help us to know your name as the servant of Yahweh and the servant of all men.

Lord, here I am; call me.

Lord, here I am; send me to be a servant to my brothers and sisters.

## 2. *The blessedness of following Christ, the Servant*

Jesus made known his intention at the time of his baptism in the Jordan. He wanted to be baptized with the crowd, together with people who, through the gift of the Holy Spirit, knew how much they were in need of God. By this gesture, he revealed his firm purpose to bear the burden of all. And when the Holy Spirit came upon him visibly, the voice of the Father was heard: 'This is my Son, my Beloved, on whom my favour rests' (Mt 3:17). It is interesting to note again the fundamental theme of the second Isaiah, that of the servant. The first song of the servant of Yahweh begins with the solemn proclamation of God: 'Here is my servant, whom I uphold, my chosen one in whom I delight' (Is 42:1).

We can live our faith in accordance with the grace and calling of baptism if we are ready to follow Christ, the Servant. Then we truly receive the good news from the Father: 'Now you have become my sons, my daughters, my chosen ones on whom my favour rests'.

In order to live with Christ, the Servant, among the lowly, the simple, the needy, we acknowledge gratefully and gladly the gift of the Holy Spirit. He alone can free us from sadness, pessimism and superficiality. Openness to the Spirit first reveals itself as a glad and grateful acceptance of the gospel, then in the courage to live the gospel, to dedicate ourselves to all who are in need and to do this, according to the gifts we have received from God, our Creator and Redeemer.

The kingdom of God is visible wherever people are no longer driven by a slavish fear but by that gratitude which is a special sign of openness to the Holy Spirit. If all our life becomes praise and thanksgiving in spirit and truthfulness, then we rejoice whenever we can use fully the gifts God has given us in view of our fellowmen. The disciple of Christ can rejoice even in the smallest things and will rejoice in his most beautiful possessions because he does not cling to them selfishly; rather, he receives them as a mission. He knows that he cannot preach the joy of the Lord unless he is ready to share with joy the gifts he has received from God. The spiritual person rejoices in the gospel in so far as he does not consider his own capacities and possessions as something to be jealously kept for himself. On the contrary, he finds true beatitude realizing how much he is indebted to his fellowmen; he then looks for every opportunity to return to them what he has received from God through them. Whoever lives in the kingdom of God the Father tends to unite people in justice, in a commitment to peace and brotherhood.

Whoever rejoices in the Lord and has found his joy in sharing, along with the gospel, all the gifts he has received, does not need too many earthly possessions. He is healthy and happy in a simple style of life, and if he occasionally experiences the hardships of life, of poverty and of service, he will not lose his equilibrium. What might lead the unbeliever to desperation becomes small for him in comparison to the joy that is already granted us and that is awaiting us if we follow Christ, the Servant. Of course, this does not preclude the right to enjoy the material goods needed for a dignified human life, especially when we can help others to take advantage of these resources for their education and human development.

A most marvellous expression of the first beatitude is found in the profound gratitude that allows us and others to accept their and our weaknesses because in others as in ourselves we discover all the good that is there, and more so yet, the power of God to bring that good to completion. Let me relate an experience that well explains this dimension.

A married woman came to me for counselling; she was very distressed. Her two children had been under psychiatric treatment and, after two and a half years, very little progress had been made. The psychiatrist had come to the conclusion that she had to divorce her husband for the sake of the children; the husband's impossible behaviour seemed to the psychiatrist to be the main cause of the children's troubles. After listening attentively to the problems presented by this lady, I recognized her inner resources and recommended the following course of action: render thanks always and everywhere; for this will constitute the path of salvation for your family. Discover your own personal resources, your endurance, your capacity to love and to accept love. She admitted that her husband still loved her although he frequently cursed and blasphemed with regard to her sexual performance; on those occasions, he would express his hatred for the Church. This had already been going on for seven years.

I further explained that 'rendering thanks to God' would include discovering more and more of the good in her husband, making herself all the more attractive to him, assisting him in discovering his own good qualities. She would also do well to recognize the good in her children by giving them credit when deserved. The lady believed in this approach and went on to put it into practice. The day before Thanksgiving Day she returned to see me; she thanked me as she brought me the good news that the miracle had happened. The husband was a new person; he had resumed going to Church with her and had even consented to adult education courses. Shortly after this, the psychiatrist informed the lady: 'Your children no longer need treatment; they are healed. However, I cannot explain how this has happened so quickly'.

The *anawim*, so beautifully represented in this woman, can face their shortcomings and those of others because of their gratitude; in praising God, they discover the good and bring it to full fruition. What great changes would happen in ourselves, in the world around us if we all stood as beggars before God and learned to appreciate and to share his gifts!

\* \* \*

Lord God, so long as we boast of our own capacities, of our own virtues and achievements, we are nothing but miserable thieves. We waste your gifts; because, where there is no gratitude, the gifts are lost. Whenever we recognize you as the source of all that is good and are ready to use your gifts in the service of our fellowmen, then we are rich; we share in the beatitude of the One who has become poor in order to make us rich. If we serve only those who can pay and reward us, we are still enslaved, but if we serve those who cannot repay us but serve out of gratitude for all you have given us, then we are well on the way to liberty.

> Lord, make us humble.
> Lord, make us free.

## 3. *The social implications*

The Church has often insisted on the social implications of the beatitudes and of the whole sermon on the mount. Pope Benedict XV, immediately after the First World War, stressed the applicability of the beatitudes to political life. Consider what would have been the consequences had the victorious and powerful nations of that time been concerned with granting to all nations a chance to live in mutual respect and freedom.

The sermon on the mount, as the law of the new covenant, leaves no room for an individualistic, narrow interpretation. We need to distinguish, though without separation, two aspects: the social outcome of a life consonant with the first beatitude and the immediate social teaching of the sermon on the mount.

Every person who lives the first beatitude with joy and conviction is a sign of the kingdom of God, a radiant light that inspires hope and spreads joy. Wherever the kingdom of God is gratefully accepted, nobody dares to exploit the poor, the handicapped, the weak; nobody yields to collective egotism. It is unthinkable for the disciples of Christ who live the first beatitude to participate in oppression, in exploitation, in racism or to evince other attitudes strikingly contradictory to that of the kingdom of love, peace and justice.

The beatitudes brought by Jesus Christ, the humble Servant, serve to comfort the poor and the oppressed even where the oppressors and the powerful social classes are not yet converts to that kingdom. The poor and the oppressed who preserve their inner peace develop their own personalities in goodness, compassion and concern for human dignity; they are truly blessed and stand as a sign of the powerful grace of God. Indeed, blessed are those who follow Christ and bear their cross; they will be a source of grace to all and will urgently plead to the rich to be converted.

However, we cannot allow ourselves to limit the Christian message to this. We should then, alas, be using the gospel to persuade the poor and the oppressed to accept their unjust situation. The gospel can be truthfully preached to the poor and the exploited only by communities of believers who are firmly committed to social justice and to peace among nations. The kingdom of God becomes visible where the disciples of Christ are guided by gratitude for the gifts of God; this means that they will use their five talents to the utmost in the service of the common good. Spiritual men who realize that everything comes from the One God and Father tend to unite their energies for the sake of creating better conditions of life: the juridical, social, cultural, economic and international agencies and structures join forces in order to honour truly the One God and Father of all.

A grateful response to the Giver of all gifts by a creative use of our capacities and earthly goods always implies service of our fellowmen. But beyond the immediate ministration to the next door neighbour, Christians who believe in the One God and Father will also become allies in their explicit commitment to justice, truthfulness and respect in socio-economic life. From that follows a new understanding of the first beatitude: blessed are those who are poor, oppressed and despised, because wherever the kingdom of God is accepted by the disciples of Christ, they not only speak of justice and peace but unite themselves so that the poor are no longer exploited and the weak no longer oppressed. We can also say: blessed are the mighty and the rich who have truly been converted to the gospel and learned to see everything as the gift of the One God and Father and are thus free from the lust for power and the desire to manipulate others.

As early as the second century, a great theologian, St Clement of Alexandria, wrote a book with the pointed question: 'Who among the rich will be saved?' He did not inquire as to whether the rich can also be saved; for there is no doubt that the kingdom of God is offered to all including those who are rich. Rather, he rightly posed the question: 'What kind of rich people can be saved?' And his answer was clear: those persons will be saved who accept the message of the kingdom of God, and therefore consider everything they possess including their capacities as entrusted to them by the Father of all for the benefit of all.

In a certain sense, priests and religious belong to the 'rich class'. They have received a good religious education; they have time to treasure up the gospel in their hearts, time to spend in the presence of Christ. But this whole spiritual wealth is given to them in view of the multitude, in view of those who have less time to pray, in view of those who do not yet know the Lord.

15

They can rejoice in this beatitude only to the extent that they make themselves the servants of their fellowmen. This equally holds true for many laymen who are privileged in the same direction. There are those who do not have to worry about their daily bread. They can foster their inner joy and beatitude to the extent that they are zealous for the kingdom of God, in the service of those who are worried and anguished.

Thus the first beatitude means reconciliation of the diversity of God's gifts with justice and brotherhood. The beatitude proclaimed by Jesus, the Servant, and shared by those who follow him, is not one of many others; rather, it is the foundation of all the beatitudes.

It is interesting to see how a great Jewish thinker comes to the same basic vision as that expressed in the life of Christ and his first beatitude. Emmanuel Levinas, a Jewish orthodox thinker who miraculously survived Hitler's camp of destruction, is a man free from all resentment. He realizes how people can grow in suffering. His main thesis is that the saving experience of God is granted to those who accept the poor man coming from below but sent from above and who allow him to impose upon them. The poor man who comes from below is any human being with nothing to offer us except his claim as a person. For Levinas, he is sent from above. He becomes the test case of whether we can honour God, the Father of all men, in the poorest of his children. The whole spirituality of Emmanuel Levinas is based on the great songs of the servant of Yahweh. And Levinas dares to ask us Christians whether we honour Jesus Christ as the One who embodies these songs in all his life. We recognize him as the servant Messiah only in as much as we honour the poor man who comes from below and recognize him thus as sent from above.

\* \* \*

Lord Jesus Christ, I adore you in your poverty for it reveals to us the richness of your love and of your beatitude. Grant, O Lord, that we may always adore you as the Servant of God the Father and the Servant of all men through our availability to our fellowmen, through humility and simplicity in the service of our brothers and sisters.

Free us, O Lord, from lust for power and from all desire to belong to a privileged class. Help us to love the poor and to appreciate their virtues. Help us to love the sufferers and cast out their miseries by the power of your love.

Grateful for your graciousness, we shall never forget that they claim, above all, respect, love and justice. What they need most is the good news, the knowledge of your name, and we can share with them this knowledge only in as much as we follow you who have come to bring the good news to the poor as a Servant of God and man.

Chapter 3

# BLESSED ARE THE SORROWFUL;
# FOR THEY SHALL FIND CONSOLATION

1. *Jesus Christ, the Consoler*

The first beatitude corresponds to the first song of the servant to whom the Father spoke first: 'you are my servant', and once he has accepted his mission as servant, the voice of the Father resounds: 'You are my Son, my Beloved'. In the second beatitude, we meet Christ as he is foretold by the second, third and fourth songs of the servant of Yahweh: 'I have laboured in vain; I have spent my strength for nothing, to no purpose; and now the Lord who formed me in the womb to be his servant . . . calls me again . . . You are my servant in whom I shall be glorified' (Is 49:4-5).

Once Peter had been inspired by the Holy Spirit, he professed his faith in Christ as the Messiah; Jesus immediately makes clear to his disciples that he is not a power Messiah but the one foretold by the prophet in the songs of the servant. He does not want his disciples to inform the people that he is the Messiah unless they understand that he is the suffering servant of God. 'From that time Jesus began to make it clear to his disciples that he had to go to Jerusalem, and there he was to suffer much from the elders, chief priests, and lawyers; he was to be put to death and to be raised again on the third day' (Mt 16:21). When Peter refuses to accept him in this role, as the man of suffering, he calls him Satan, a tempter, a stumbling

19

block. We cannot gather around Christ and receive a share in his beatitude unless we recognize him as the servant who suffers for his people.

Jesus is able to console us because he does not turn away from us in the hour of suffering. 'The Lord has given me the tongue of a teacher and skill to console the weary with a word; each morning he wakes me to hear that I might listen like one who is taught. The Lord God opened my ears and I did not disobey or turn back in defiance. I offered my back to the lash, and let my beard be plucked from my chin, I did not hide my face from spitting and insult' (Is 50:4-6).

If we want to gather around Christ, we must meet under his cross with gratitude, in full awareness that he bore our burdens. 'Yet ours were the sufferings he bore, our torments he endured.... He was pierced for our transgressions.... The chastisement he bore is health for us and by his scourging we are healed' (Is 53:4-5).

Christ is not only the servant to whom the Father reveals his secrets because of his acceptance of the poor coming from below and sent from above, but he is ready to allow the poor to impose upon him. The mystery is even greater in that he allows his enemies, like us who, by our sins, become his enemies, to impose upon him. He considers the miseries of the sinful world part of the mission of his life; he bears our cross. His passion and death are a blessed event and beatitude for they are the greatest manifestation of the compassion of the heavenly Father for all of us, a compassion that brings consolation and redemption if we consent to gather under the cross of Christ.

In his passion and in his unlimited readiness to bear our burden, Jesus is the perfect image of the heavenly Father. That is why he can invite us in the sermon on the mount: 'There must be no limit to your goodness, as your heavenly Father's goodness knows no bounds' (Mt 5:48). In the shorter version of the sermon on the mount, St Luke translates these words in the light of the passion and compassion of Christ: 'Be compassionate just as your heavenly Father is compassionate' (Lk 6:36). When Philip asked Jesus: 'Lord, show us the Father and it will suffice', Jesus answered: 'Anyone who has seen me has seen the Father' (Jn 14:8-9). Jesus addresses us in these words while in his infinite compassion he is about to go to bear our burden on the cross.

Christ did not come to seek his own pleasure and his own glory; that is why he is never beset by sorrow because of self-interest or personal concern. His affliction is blessed because it always marks the supreme sign of divine and human love; it is a sacrament of the compassion of the heavenly Father, the fullest manifestation of saving solidarity with all of us.

When the suffering, the passion and compassion of Jesus reached their summit at the Mount of Olives where his sweat was like drops of blood falling to the ground, 'there appeared to him an angel from heaven bringing him consolation and strength' (Lk 22:43-44). The angel did not come to free him from suffering, but the coming is the sign of the Father's presence that gives him strength, and opens on to the horizon of the final beatitude. So it becomes evident that the compassion of Jesus Christ is the fullest possible participation in the compassion and the beatitude of the heavenly Father. Consolation is never wanting in the heart of Jesus, not even in the agonizing pain on the cross, because he accepts the cup of suffering from the hands of the Father knowing that it will be, for all of us, the cup of salvation. He did not go to seek his own glory but that of the Father and he knows that the Father will glorify him. While he makes known to us the infinite compassion of the Father and thus the name of the Father, he can pray: 'Father, glorify your Son that the Son may glorify you' (Jn 17:1).

The great promise and pledge of the final beatitude is the risen Lord who shows us the wounds of his hands and heart open for our salvation. These are the great signs of those who follow Christ; whoever is ready to gather round him under the cross will experience final consolation.

Faith in the resurrection is a source of strength that draws us and even compels us to gather under the cross of Christ. But it is equally true that only if one has the courage to stand under the cross will one come to that deep experience of God in joy which is at the very heart of our faith in the resurrection.

\* \* \*

21

Lord Jesus Christ, you have called your disciples to gather around you on the mount of the beatitudes; you have called your privileged disciples to Mount Tabor with a view to preparing them to follow you on to Mount Calvary. Many failed you when you went up to Mount Calvary to proclaim your new law of love, a love that is tested in suffering. Lord, give us the courage to gather around you on Mount Calvary; then can we be sure that we are called to the mount of eternal beatitude.

Blessed are we if we meet you and your cross through a sincere sorrow for our own sins and compassion for our fellow-men; a sorrow that unites us with you is always a blessed way to consolation in the Holy Spirit.

Blessed are we if we no longer experience sadness because of selfishness or selfish motives. This is possible only if sorrow for our sins and compassion for the misery of the sinful world totally take hold of us as we stand under your cross, O Lord.

## 2. *Gathered around Christ*

From a psychological point of view, it is evident that we cannot truly rejoice and experience a profound consolation if we cannot suffer in truthful compassion with our fellowmen. The famous ethologist Konrad Lorenz, Nobel prize-winner for his studies on the social behaviour of animals, reveals that he is also a great therapist when he asserts in his book, *The Eight Deadly Sins of Modern Man,* that one of the most deadly behaviours is man's incapacity to suffer with others and for others. Those who are unwilling or unable to suffer in active compassion with others are also unable to share their joys; indeed, they will be unable to rejoice because it is not possible to experience deep joy without sharing it with others. The touchstone of our capacity to open ourselves to blessed sorrow is our readiness to bear the burden of others. It is so very easy to express sorrow about the unhappiness and distresses of others; indeed, it is somewhat of a lie to express compassion if we are not willing to suffer with them and for them.

St Paul distinguishes clearly the affliction that aligns us

with the sinful and frustrated world from the sorrow that is the bearer of salvation: 'The wound which is borne in God's way brings a change of heart too salutary to regret; but the hurt which is born in the way of the selfish world brings death' (2 Cor 7:10).

There are many sad, frustrated and sour people for whom the Lord's blessing and beatitude is not available because of their self-centredness and apathy that lock them into their little ego and separate them from the loving human community and from Christ's own beatitude. Even sorrow for our sins cannot be authentic as long as we close our heart whenever faced with the misery and suffering of other people. The motives and the quality of our affliction and sadness are a mirror of our inner value. What are we saying about ourselves when we have sleepless nights because someone has contradicted us or misunderstood our motives while we sleep easily disregarding the enormous suffering of hundreds and of millions of hungry people, the many oppressed and exploited persons and groups? What a contradiction if a Christian is sad because someone is unwilling to dance around him, while he feels no deep pain for the white minority in Rhodesia and South Africa who are refusing the most basic human rights to people because they are black and poor.

How unhappy and self-degrading are those wealthy people who are seeking ever new ways to indulge in luxury, to unite themselves to the joyless groups and classes fighting for privileges; they are truly the most miserable people in the world. Because they are unconcerned about others and refuse to bear a little bit of the burden of others, they have closed themselves totally to the joy that comes from God and leads to God.

Very different is the sorrow that manifests the coming of the kingdom of God; it is a profound sorrow for our sin because it causes suffering not only for ourselves but for others as well.

Blessed are those who, after each sin, turn immediately to God with an act of sorrow and great trust. This was one of the practices of Pope John XXIII: 'After each sin, I shall turn to God with an act of sorrow and great, great trust; and then: "John, go ahead as if Jesus has given you a kiss".' He was a

23

man who could be sorrowful with the suffering and consequently could rejoice with the joyful. He experienced that profound consolation that arises from trust in God after a sincere act of sorrow.

When, after each fall, man turns to God sincerely and trustfully, he fears little the misery of sin in his own heart and in the world around him; he who expresses his sorrow before the Lord will also readily humble himself before his brothers and sisters to whom he has been unjust because of his sin. Those who learn to gather under the cross of Christ will not so much be sad because of the poor impression they have made but rather because they have offended God and have deprived their fellowmen of the light, warmth, kindness and justice they should have provided them.

Many good intentions never find expression in practice because people have not purified their heart by a sincere act of sorrow, and therefore they have not put their trust in God, who heals and gives strength. There is no way of translating intention into practice without putting to death our selfishness, and learning to bear the cross for our benefit and that of others. On the contrary, purposes that arise from a deep sorrow that unites us with the blessed passion and compassion of Christ will be effective. Self-denial and a courageous 'no' to collective selfishness brings sorrow; however, it is a sorrow that already bears in itself the joy and the power of the risen Lord.

\* \* \*

Lord Jesus Christ, I thank you for inviting me to go up the Mount and to stand under your cross in union with my brothers and sisters. I thank you for the great manifestation of your love and the compassion you showed all of us. But all too often when you called me to come up the Mount of Calvary and to stand face-to-face with your cross, I was unwilling to do so and fell into sadness instead of a blessed sorrow, not so much because I had offended the Father and you or humiliated my brothers; I was afflicted and angry because others had not done my will. I was frustrated because I projected an unfavourable image. If all this happened, it is that I have not yet learned to stand near you under the cross. Yet, I praise you; for again and again I have experienced the beatitude of those who are sorrowful with you for the cause of your kingdom.

## 3. *The social implications*

Every sin has an appalling social aspect. Whenever we neglect to do the good that we could and should do, we deprive the world of that light, truth and strength to which it is entitled. Whoever indulges in an evil he could avoid increases the misery and slavery brought into the world by sin. The sorrow that arises from God's grace and leads us to the cross of the Lord has an even greater social power. The true believer is pained by his sin for it has decreased salvation not only in him but also in the world around him. If he had followed faithfully the grace of God and had made the best use of all the gifts God had entrusted to him, he would have been a source of salvation, of goodness, health, benevolence, joy and justice.

Each time we are unfaithful to God's calling, we become sad in a way that is opposed to the beatitude granted those who are truly sorrowful. The sorrow of the believer is not so much a regret for having lost an occasion to gain merit; rather, it deplores the injustice done to God's honour and to the community around him. And so in each authentic act of sorrow, there is at least a beginning of a renewed love for the heavenly Father, and at the same time a new beginning of love and justice towards fellowmen, a new solidarity of salvation.

The renewed liturgy of the sacrament of reconciliation can greatly help us to discover the social implications of sorrow, of reconciliation and of conversion. The experience that God accepts us as we are should make us willing to stand together under his cross and be grateful that we are accepted by him. We can then accept each other and honour our common vocation to bear one another's burdens.

The communal celebration of conversion, of healing forgiveness and renewal does not exclude our readiness to confess our personal sins both in a sacramental setting and in our daily life. The purpose of the liturgical renewal is to overcome the dichotomy between liturgy and life. If we meditate together on the Lord's compassion and blessed passion, and if we truly stand under the cross of the Lord, we shall commit ourselves to a common effort for renewal. We all know that personal conversion as well as ecclesial and social renewal demand a great deal of self-denial and willingness to suffer.

Whoever has a deep experience, in faith, of the social implications of each sin and of the horrifying solidarity of perdition will be deeply shaken and will suffer. However, it will give him an even deeper appreciation and greater experience of the solidarity of salvation. Conversion will then be a recommitment to this saving solidarity in Jesus Christ.

A total dedication to the apostolate is unavoidably a share in Christ's suffering. The apostle of the Gentiles speaks with moving words about this experience: 'Hard pressed on every side, we are never hemmed in; bewildered, we are never at our wits' end; hunted, we are never abandoned to our fate; struck down, we are not left to die. Wherever we go we carry death with us in our body, the death that Jesus died, that in this body also life may reveal itself, the life that Jesus lives. For continually, while still alive, we are being surrendered into the hands of death, for Jesus' sake, so that the life of Jesus may also be revealed in this mortal body of ours. Thus death is at work in us, and life in you' (2 Cor 4:8-12). Paul was many a time faced with death; he had to meet dangers from rivers, from robbers and even from his fellow-countrymen, dangers at sea and from false friends. Yet, Paul finds his joy and pride in the very things that are his weakness (2 Cor 11:23-12:9).

In our own lifetime, we have seen the great pioneers of non-violent liberation, men like Martin Luther King and Mahatma Gandhi. They worked and were strikingly blessed under the sign of the cross. Their commitment to justice and brotherhood, their effort to free mankind from violent oppression brought suffering, but they were able to radiate the beatitude and consolation which Christ proclaimed on the mount of the beatitudes.

Where the kingdom of God is accepted and people are converted to Christ, there will be many blessings for the afflicted, for the sorrowful, for the lonely, for the sick and for the imprisoned. Whoever is committed to this kingdom will never forget those who are particularly signed by the cross of Jesus. Where there are truthful followers of Christ who are willing to follow him to the mount of the beatitudes and to Mount Calvary, their old people will no longer live in desperate loneliness. They will find visitors; they will find someone to manifest love and concern.

In one who has experienced the consolation given to those who are sorrowful for their sins, there will arise the works of mercy meant to overcome the most frustrating thorns of sadness and loneliness. If we are truly believers, we shall bring consolation to the needy in our neighbourhood and unite our energies to help the countless people throughout the world who are suffering from famine, earthquakes and other catastrophes.

Whoever has come to know Christ, the Consoler, and the grace of the Spirit will do his best to spread the gospel not merely by words but by that total witness marking people as a living gospel. Blessed are those who after being healed from their sins are consolers; they will be a blessing for many who, without the gospel, would live in darkness and despair.

The nearness of the Lord to his disciples is the main source of consolation. We experience Christ's nearness when we are gathered in his name for praise and thanksgiving, and in the desire to know him better, to follow him more truthfully. Christ promised his presence to those who are consecrated to the service of his gospel. We should not forget other forms in which Christ meets us and offers us the opportunity to be with him. He comes to us under the disguise of the poor, the hungry. There he is with us as the One crucified for us but also the One who is our judge if we refuse him as our Saviour. 'For when I was hungry, you gave me food; when thirsty, you gave me drink; when I was a stranger you took me into your home, when naked you clothed me; when I was ill you came to my help, when in prison you visited me. . . . I tell you this: anything you did for one of my brothers, however humble, you did it

27

for me' (Mt 25:35-50). Blessed are we if we discover this real though hidden presence of Christ crucified, the Christ who forces a decision upon us as to whether we will meet him as Saviour or as Judge.

As Christians, we should all be united in the one, holy, Catholic and apostolic Church if we gather around Christ under his cross. The triumphalism of the self-righteous or the collective arrogance that scattered Christians and divided the Church of Christ will then be overcome. If we love Christ, we suffer from these divisions and from all sin causing that division. There is no way to experience the joy of Christian unity other than to gather together under the cross of the Lord, to repent together and to commit ourselves together to pray and to suffer for the cause of Christian unity. Then we shall again and again experience consolation. Christ is with us through his Paraclete.

\* \* \*

Lord Jesus Christ, great is my desire to have a share in your Easter joy and equally I am longing to bring this joy and beatitude to my brothers and sisters. But alas, I have so often failed in courage and readiness to be with you under your cross. Therefore, I have not yet fully integrated within me your compassion for all men.

Forgive me, Lord. Heal me, for I have sinned.

Let your Holy Spirit come upon me to cleanse me. Grant me a heart renewed that I may recognize the evil of sin and learn to accept the daily cross that is part of my commitment to justice and peace, to spreading your gospel. In the celebration of your sacraments as in daily life, open my eyes that I may see with your merciful eyes as you looked at the crowd.

Let us be so gathered around you, that we share your compassion and your readiness to suffer for our fellowmen and thus become a living gospel.

# Chapter 4

# BLESSED ARE THOSE OF GENTLE SPIRIT; THEY SHALL HAVE THE EARTH FOR THEIR POSSESSION

## 1. *The gentle Christ*

Christ is gentleness in person and gentleness is the harvest of the Spirit. Anointed by the Spirit and filled with beatitude, Jesus the Servant is ready to bear the burden of all men. He sees gentleness as the way to conquer the hearts of people and to redeem the world. The first song of the servant pointed to this particular aspect of the mission of Christ. 'He will not call out or lift his voice high or make himself heard in the open street. He will not break a bruised reed, or snuff out a smouldering wick. ... He will plant justice on earth' (Is 42:2-4).

Looking to the intimidated, oppressed and anguished crowd, Jesus calls his disciples to gather around him and learn gentleness from him as well as kindness, goodness and benevolence. He bespeaks gentleness; more yet, he radiates it. If we truly gather around him, together we shall become, in him and through him, a sacrament of gentleness. 'Come to me, all whose work is hard, whose load is heavy; and I will give you relief. Bend your necks to my yoke, and learn from me; for I am gentle and humble-hearted' (Mt 11:28-29).

Christ did not come to subdue the world by the sword. And he disappointed many Jews, high-priests, priests and even some of his relatives by his refusal to be a power-Messiah. He discerns the attractive power of kindness and gentleness and he believes, as no one else before him or after him can, that we are created in God's image and likeness and that we can be liberated and transfigured by the gentleness of his love. There is no manipulation in Christ's relationship with his disciples and the crowd. His pedagogy is dialogic and liberating because it is patient and gentle. He appeals by his life and death, by his word and radiant personality, to the heart and mind of the people; he thereby awakens the response of a sincere conscience. Whoever believes in him, abides with him on the mount of the beatitudes and under his cross will experience the winning power of his goodness and will therefore want to respond in great freedom and with grateful joy.

The gospel gives us innumerable examples of Christ's most gentle sensitivity towards different kinds of people. How wonderful is his gentleness and even reverence when he receives the woman who was known all over town as a sinner (Lk 7: 26-49). The Servant of God makes her a new person through his respect and his kindness. He gives her credit from the very beginning and foretells that she will love him with a pure and strong love. He has acted in a similar way with many other persons.

Christ is the great sacrament of God's goodness by his gentleness. His deep experience of union with the Father gives him the most perfect consciousness of solidarity with all of mankind. A glance at the behaviour of the disciples whom Christ called to gather around him is revealing; without fail, he displays unlimited patience when confronted with their rude and arrogant incomprehension. Again and again their dispute centres on who is the greatest among them; they thus distance themselves from Jesus who is the sacrament of gentleness and humility. Yet, he waits for them, calls them, and teaches them over and over again by example and words. Constant forbearance and gentleness typify the behaviour of Jesus when he is faced with so much stupidity and ingratitude on the part of those he called to be his friends. We can only be astonished at this unheard-of miracle. How great must be his beatitude for him to

30

be so patient and gentle with them! He kindly addresses the priests and the Pharisees and tries to convince them by his absolute sincerity and astonishing gentleness. Even when his apostle Judas comes to betray him with a kiss, he utters the most cordial word: 'Friend'. There is surely no irony or sarcasm in his word; it is the last attempt and most wonderful effort of Jesus' gentleness to win over the heart of Judas.

In his hour of extreme pain and suffering, Jesus remains concerned for all those around him; he consoles with gentle words the women who weep over him, and he assures the brigand crucified with him of his abiding friendship. But the culmination of his gentleness comes in his prayer for those who crucify him: 'Father, forgive them'.

Jesus continues to be patient and gentle and he is convinced of final victory. Through his gentleness, he will draw all people to himself, and he wants to pursue this work through his disciples.

\* \* \*

Father, Lord of heaven and earth, we praise you for having revealed your own patience and gentleness in Jesus Christ, your Servant, your beloved Son. Open our eyes that we may look at him, that we may know him in his gentleness, trust in him and learn from him.

## 2. *Gathered around Christ*

Jesus went up the mount and his disciples gathered around him. It is the privilege of believers to go up the mount with Jesus, to stay near him and to allow him to radiate his goodness and gentleness. But we can never forget that in view of the multitude, it is a privilege also to learn from Jesus and to receive from him the gift of gentleness, graciousness and non-violence; they are a fundamental condition for our apostolate and social commitment.

Patience and gentleness, however, must not be misunderstood

as a kind of inertia or laziness. In the best Catholic tradition, gentleness, patience and non-violence are considered the most noble part of the virtue of fortitude. They point to the insuperable energies of love, benevolence and respect for others; they constitute that specific strength that gathers all the energies of the heart, the emotions, the intellect, the will and all our passions into a firm commitment to the gospel of justice, peace and love. By his example and explicit words, Jesus tells us that the only way to attract people to his kingdom is that of patience and gentleness. We can never serve God's kingdom and build up a brotherly and peaceful world without the firm character and fundamental attitudes of patience and gentleness; we are not allowed to dissipate our precious energies so needed for our service to the brethren.

Blessed are we if by our kindness, benevolence, reverence and gentleness we can convince people that the kingdom of God has come, that Christ, exalted on the cross and exultant in his resurrection, attracts all people to his heart. If we know Christ in his gentleness, and treasure up his gospel in our hearts, then we can communicate our belief that conversion to gentleness and non-violence is possible.

He who truly believes in Christ, the humble servant, and in the power of the Holy Spirit, will never use such means as speech, writing or actions to degrade others. An old German proverb says: 'Friend, you are wrong for you are rude'. Gentleness, on the contrary, is one of the most unmistakable signs that we are guided by the Spirit of Christ, that we live in his truth. 'If you are guided by the Spirit, you will not fulfil the desires of your selfish self. . . . But the harvest of the Spirit is love, joy, peace, patience, kindness, goodness, fidelity, gentleness and self-control' (Gal 5 : 16-22).

We read in the four holy books of Confucius: 'The four greatest gifts which heaven has bestowed on wise people are: benevolence, gentleness, justice and prudence'. In a manner similar to the gospels', Confucius explains how benevolence and reverence for others manifest themselves by gentleness; if we truly love and respect our fellowmen, we find spontaneously the right expressions in our relationship to them. The great Chinese pedagogue insists that one cannot display patience as a tactic or learn gentleness before the mirror because they are the harvest and visible sign of benevolence and reverence. Hence, gentleness mirrors the pure heart. In this vision, Confucius comes close to Christ and we can all rejoice that the Spirit of Christ has prompted such insights all over the world.

The New Testament often insists on the necessity of fraternal correction. However, as Christ and the apostles teach us, such assistance cannot be offered by people who continually grumble and indulge in sour criticism. Whoever wants to fulfil this spiritual work of mercy must first of all learn from Christ's gentleness to express profound respect and benevolence. After having exalted gentleness and benevolence as harvest of the Spirit, Paul speaks of fraternal correction. 'We must not be conceited, challenging one another to rivalry, jealous of one another. If a man should do something wrong, my brothers, on a sudden impulse, you who are endowed with the Spirit must set him right again very gently. Look to yourself, each one of you: you may be tempted too. Help one another to carry these heavy loads, and in this way you will fulfil the law of Christ' (Gal 6:1-2). In this text, the centrality of gentleness is clear; it is at the very heart of the law of Christ. We cannot express our saving solidarity with each other without this firm attribute of gentleness.

The great doctors of the Church, such as St Albert the Great and St Thomas Aquinas, considered fraternal correction one of the forms of the sacrament of reconciliation. They did not want to diminish the importance of the private confession to the priest but neither did they allow the confessional function to be severed from life. They clearly set the condition under which fraternal correction can acquire a sacramental significance and become a sign of Christ's gracious presence among us. We are truly gathered in the name of Jesus and experience his saving presence to the extent first, that we offer fraternal correction with great gentleness and come to accept it from others with similar gentleness, and second, that we unite ourselves in prayer before Christ whose gentleness attracts us, heals us and forgives us. We pray him to make us of gentle spirit, his messengers and channels of his peace.

I consider important the declaration of the Second Vatican Council on religious liberty in the light of this beatitude. It is an appeal to all believers to win over the earth for Christ, for themselves and for the Church by their witness of reverence and gentleness in the spirit of the gospel. Indeed, if all our way of thinking, speaking and acting is permeated by evangelical gentleness, then it is absurd to resort to discrimination, to manipulation, or to the secular arm in order to force people to submit to the institutional Church. Only those who manifest this spirit of gentleness are guided by the Spirit of truth. A bishop of Latin America expressed this attitude in a personal conversation with me. In his humility, he felt that he was unable to judge the inner value of the various theological currents in the documents presented to the council. However, he admitted having based his decisions on the gentleness and respect with which one section of the Council Fathers addressed the questions. He thus followed gentleness as a fundamental sign of discernment and he did so rightly.

\* \* \*

Lord Jesus Christ, you have not only spoken of gentleness to your disciples on the mount of the beatitudes. You have made it visible on Mount Calvary and on all occasions when you were in the midst of your disciples. You have radiated this wonderful gift by your life and continue to do so by the mission of the Holy Spirit. Let your Holy Spirit come upon us that we may be transformed into visible signs of your own gentleness. Make us messengers of truth; free us from false confidence in our own strength; never allow us to place our hope in any form of earthly power.

Lord, make us patient.
Lord, make us gentle.

## 3. *The social implications*

The social relevance of the evangelical spirit of gentleness is obvious. Human relationships, especially in the economic, cultural, social, political and international realms, are frequently envenomed by bitter criticism, by violence, by debasing manipulation. This is due to the fact that gentleness, fruit of benevolence and mutual respect, is lacking.

Disciples who are truly gathered around Christ and who come to know him gratefully as gentleness incarnate, have the distinct mission to permeate their *milieu* with the spirit of gentleness and discernment; the task is fulfilled solely by those who display benevolence and gentleness in their personal life. The multitude suffering so terribly under terrorism, disregard, manipulation and other forms of violence, urgently need genuine disciples of Christ to create an atmosphere of respect, benevolence, gentleness and non-violent action for justice and peace.

A social contribution of paramount importance is a constructive and gentle dialogue with a view to fostering a healthy public opinion. For instance, if we cannot agree with the type of television programming available or with editorials in the daily newspapers and magazines, we should not express dissent by rude letters; more will be gained by exquisite expressions of gentleness. If we try to dissuade the directors of television stations from showing so much violence, we are likely to fail if we resort to violent and rude language. If there is need to express criticism, it will surely be more effective if we express our discontent in the form of a gentle question or with convincing arguments devoid of harsh words. Healthy and constructive criticism is surely needed, but we need positive action in the form of encouragement and appreciation of good programmes.

Some years ago, I had to counsel a religious who displayed a general tendency to protest all too frequently; he had come to the point of being very bitter and angry. I suggested to him, as penance, to abstain for half a year from all negative comments of concern to his own community, from criticism of the hierarchy and, if possible, from any censorious expression. He accepted the advice literally and a few months later he told me: 'I no longer need to express vitriolic criticism because my *confrères* and my superiors seek my advice and pay attention to it'.

Not all ardent disciples of Christ have a political vocation although I do hope that the politically adept, like Robert Schumann, will follow their calling and make a contribution to the reconciliation of nations and social classes. All believers can and should influence their culture; their value system should come to bear on the political life of their community by their fostering of the spirit of gentleness and non-violence.

Mahatma Gandhi, one of the greatest Christians of our era, had no distinct religious or institutional affiliation; yet, he has given us a unique model of non-violent action. He gathered his friends in his ashrams, that is, his houses of prayer, where together they meditated on the beatitudes, the gospel of non-violence. The great master of non-violent liberation was convinced that without a spirit of contemplation, all non-violent techniques become psychological violence or manipulations. He felt that without a spirit of contemplation we unavoidably become manipulative manipulators. The purpose of his ashrams and of his life of contemplation was to reach out for that perfect consciousness of union with God that leads to an equally conscious solidarity with all men, with the whole of creation. It is the main recourse for strong, patient and convincing non-violent action.

Let us also be mindful of the fact that for Mahatma Gandhi, his genuine witness to non-violence would have been impossible without an ardent zeal for social justice and peace on all levels. Non-violence lies in the great power of truth, not truths discussed but the truth lived in solidarity with all men. Non-violent liberating action occasionally becomes a very courageous confrontation to unmask hypocrisy and injustice. It will be truly non-violent and liberating if we help those we have to reprove or oppose, if we assist them in discovering their inner resources of goodness and justice, if we believe in the almighty power of God's love and in the good will of most people; we are then able to join hands for a concerted action.

I hold the conviction that the charismatic renewal has great potentiality for the fostering of non-violent action. The praise of God in all events of life helps us discover and acknowledge gladly the good in all men, and especially in those who descend upon us with impositions. Many people actively involved in charismatic prayer groups indulged earlier in bitter criticism; they have not renounced discernment, but when they must express criticism, they do so gently and with respect for the person criticized. This is surely a great step forward. We should not allow ourselves to disparage charismatic renewal on the basis that it has not yet organized many forms of social action. It is very important that after such a short time, the movement has manifested a capacity to transform persons in conformity with the spirit of gentleness. But I also hope that, in time, there will arise very explicit movements towards solidarity, non-violent action for a more healthy, brotherly and peaceful society and world.

Those who have a hard time accepting the message of non-violent action often refer to the actions of Jesus when he purged the temple of misuse of religion. 'Jesus made a whip of cords and drove them out of the temple, sheep, cattle and all. . . . Then he turned on the dealers in pigeons: "Take them out", he said, "You must not turn my Father's house into a market" ' (Jn 2: 14-16). The other gospels do not mention a whip of cords, but simply that Jesus drove them all out. There is no evidence to prove that Jesus actually scourged anyone in the temple. But there is no doubt about his wrath against false religion. Only if the Church truly becomes a house of prayer and if we all learn to adore God in truthfulness, is there hope that our wrath will not be a useless explosion of energies; instead, let us collect all our energies in gentle but strong actions for the liberation of all people in justice and peace.

\* \* \*

Lord Jesus Christ, when you invite us to gather around you and to rejoice with you, let us never forget the multitude of people who are oppressed, exploited and manipulated. Fill us with zeal for justice and peace and teach us to be humble and of gentle spirit.

Forgive me, O Lord, for so frequently engaging in debates and useless dissent. I have failed to be a mirror-image of you. Often I have not made a genuine effort to reflect your respect for and gentleness to my brothers and sisters. Unfortunately, I have often tried to impose my own way of thinking on others instead of first listening to them. What could have been a dialogue of faith and of mutual evangelization has frequently degenerated into useless discussions because of my own lack of gentleness and respect. Thus have I missed so many occasions to win over my brothers and the world around me to the kingdom of your peace, to your reign of benevolence and gentleness.

Send forth your Spirit and grant to us a heart renewed; grant us a new spirit, a spirit of gentleness and non-violent commitment.

Chapter 5

# BLESSED ARE THOSE WHO HUNGER
# AND THIRST FOR GOD'S JUSTICE;
# THEY SHALL BE SATISFIED

## 1. *Christ, embodiment of the new justice*

Christ invites us to follow him in the presence of the crowd
and to be gathered around him so as to learn from him who
hungers and thirsts for the Father's justice to prevail. He
teaches us this new, saving justice on Mount Calvary as much
as on the mount of the beatitudes. Christ did not come to seek
his own glory; it is his great hunger and thirst to see the
heavenly Father honoured and glorified by all men, to see him
honoured by a more brotherly and equitable human society.
From the beginning of his human life to his exaltation on the
cross, Christ had no greater desire than to teach the world how
to respond to the wonderful justice which the Father manifested
in him, and to see all human relationships mirror this new
justice. In the eyes of Jesus, all ritual sacrifices without justice
count for little, and therefore, he offers himself totally to the
service of his brethren; he gives himself fully to the honour of
the Father so that in the world justice may prevail.

The first song of the servant of Yahweh depicts the justice
that will come with the Messiah. 'He will make justice shine
in truth; he will neither rebuke nor wound; he will plant justice

on earth, while coasts and islands wait for his teaching'
(Is 42:3-4).

A personal knowledge of Christ precedes the understanding
of that justice of which he speaks. Christ is the embodiment or
the incarnation of the new justice that comes from heaven. It is
the justice of God, the Almighty Father, Love almighty who,
after having created man in his image and likeness, cannot
abandon him to the misery of sin. Sinful men hold no title to
reconciliation or to re-introduction into the great honour of
being God's chosen children. But it is God as Father, who
for his own name's sake, cannot give us up; in justice to himself,
he is obliged to care for the weakest of his creatures, for those
who cannot help themselves. In every good family, the father
and all other members of the family give special attention and
assistance to those who are weakest. This paternal love is only
a pale image of God's justice. Christ is the perfect sacrament,
the consummate visible sign of the justice of the heavenly
Father. This reality inspires great trust and joy if we accept the
new law of justice from Jesus Christ.

Jesus' whole life and death supremely manifest God's
merciful, compassionate justice. Christ feels compelled from
within to make God's saving justice fully visible. Jesus Christ,
true man and truly our brother, has received the greatest possible
gift from the Father: divine sonship. His human nature is
singularly united with the Eternal Word of the Father, with the
only-begotten Son of the Father. This unique gift to his human
nature is bestowed with a view to the salvation of all mankind,
and so Jesus, in justice, feels obliged to give himself totally to
the service of his brothers and sisters. Therefore, he hungers
and thirsts to establish the new direction of justice on earth by
his life and in his blood.

Jesus makes a surprising pronouncement about this justice
at the time of his baptism in the Jordan with the rest of the
crowd (cf. Lk 3:21). John the Baptist is shocked to learn that
Jesus wants to be baptized with people who knew their need for
God. But Jesus answers: 'Let it be so for the present; we do
well to conform in this way with all of God's justice' (Mt 3:15).
Specially in the gospel of St Matthew and in the letters of

St Paul, the word *dikaiosyne* takes on an extremely profound meaning. It becomes particularly evident when Jesus considers his baptism with the crowd as an exigency of the Father's justice; and Jesus uses the same word in the beatitudes. The justice of which he speaks and which he embodies in his life and death is that of the Father and of the Son who has freely chosen to be the brother of all men to the honour of the Father. His baptism in the Jordan is only the introit and the promise of the baptism in blood which he will receive for all of us on his cross. The blood of the new and everlasting covenant is the strongest and most visible expression of the justice of the heavenly Father and of the new brotherly justice that will reign on earth. Jesus truly hungers and thirsts for the Father's rightful rule of saving solidarity to dwell on earth, in the heart of all people and in all their relationships. So Jesus said, in fulfilment of the scriptures: 'I thirst' (Jn 19:28).

Jesus calls his disciples to Mount Calvary as he did to the mount of the beatitudes so that they may share in his hunger and thirst for this new justice. We, his disciples, are truly his Church if, in and through our life, we make visible to all men this hunger and thirst for justice.

\* \* \*

Lord Jesus Christ, I thank you for crying out on the cross: 'I thirst'. You are thirsty for my response to the astounding saving justice you have shown to all men including me. By your new justice, by your hunger and thirst for it to reign among us, you have shown us the Father. Send us the Holy Spirit that we may be transfigured with you, that we may no longer be restless and afflicted because of our limited concern for our narrow justice. I admit my sin: my selfish concern for my own justice, for my little rights; thus have I become an obstacle to your saving justice. But when inspired by the Holy Spirit, I pray to hunger and thirst for your justice in all events and all conditions of my life and that of my fellowmen, then shall I know better how to become a sign of your justice and find the proper criteria for my desires, for my purposes, my work and my actions.

## 2. *The disciples gathered around Christ*

The most privileged disciple of Christ, the one who is closest to him in his beatitudes and under the cross is Mary, his mother. Throughout her life she sings of that hunger and thirst for the new justice proclaimed by Jesus Christ. 'The hungry he has satisfied with good things, the rich he has sent empty away' (Lk 1:53). In and through Jesus Christ, Mary stands as the queen of prophets as she relates the greatness of the Lord who unthrones the arrogant and exalts the humble. The biblical image of Mary as disciple of Christ or Mary as prophet differs significantly from that of the 'apparitions' and visions reported in Italy, where here concerns centre on dress or trivia. The disciples of Christ and the true venerators of Mary, the great devotee of Christ, are known by their hunger and thirst for God's saving justice in all human relationships.

If we truly come together under the cross and gather around Christ on the mount of the beatitudes, depending on the Spirit he sends to us from above, then we shall no longer be worried about small things but shall be unfettered from individual and group selfishness. Through our faith in Jesus, we shall be transformed into signs of his presence, of his hunger and thirst for the rightful rule of the Father who takes care of the weak and the poor, the oppressed and the exploited. Through faith and baptism we enter into God's family and consequently into the saving justice Christ made visible on earth. We believe in God, the Father Almighty, and therefore have the courage to put to death our selfishness and to commit ourselves to the recognition and fostering of every man's dignity. In baptism, we are justified by faith through God's grace alone. Thus we have an inner share in Christ's wonderful justice as he lived it and brought it on earth. If we are gratuitously accepted by God, if he has given us Jesus Christ and in him the blood of the covenant, then we can no longer live selfishly for ourselves

42

but must live for Christ who died for us. So the very justification by God's grace becomes a *leitmotiv* for the disciples of Christ to be committed to God's saving justice; Christ pledged himself at his baptism, he who came in water, in blood and in the Holy Spirit.

Baptism brought us into the one great family of God where each, according to his share in God's gifts, is concerned about those who are in need. If we believe in the baptism of Christ and in our share of it, then we cannot consider earthly goods, our professional qualifications and special charisms as if they were our own property, to be used for our own convenience. We can receive them and preserve them in justice before God only if we look to those whom we can serve, to those who most need our service.

We can celebrate the Eucharist in the kingdom of God, which is the realm of love, of justice and of peace, and we can be transformed through the ongoing praise of God to the extent that we share the word of God as well as our daily bread by co-operating with others on all levels so as to reveal ourselves as members of God's family in Jesus Christ. I once met two families in extreme misery and I approached a wealthy Catholic for generous and immediate help. He responded by: 'I really do not see why I should because no one has ever done anything for me'. Since I am persistent, I pursued my goal as follows: 'You must truly be the poorest and most miserable man since you have not yet discovered that your wealth is the result of the work and conscientiousness of so many other people; it may be that you are yet an unbeliever since you arrogantly say that you have received nothing from anyone; you therefore snatch honour and steal all your property from God'. The man understood and changed his mind.

If we gather around Christ in the celebration of reconciliation, we shall then discover that the real sins are those against justice and peace among people and among social classes. It is inconceivable that we should receive the word of forgiveness with gratitude while refusing to learn from Jesus to hunger and thirst for justice on all levels. Indeed, if we examine our conscience, one of the inevitable questions will be: 'Do we

43

truly share in Christ's hunger and thirst for the new justice that unites all people in mutual respect and in concern for those who are most in need?'

* * *

We believe in one God, the Father Almighty; we therefore believe that we can be transformed and converted so as to become a sign of his concern for all his children.

— Lord, we believe in you; we praise your Fatherly justice.

We believe that the one God and Father made all things visible and invisible. We truly believe this when, generously and spontaneously, we place all our capacities in the service of the common good.

— Lord, we believe in you; we praise your Fatherly justice.

We believe that the Father has shared everything with us. He spoke his wisdom and love in his Word and he shares his eternal Word with us in Jesus who is justice incarnate. If we believe this, then we shall be one family concerned for each other and respectful of each other, thus proclaiming our faith.

— Lord, we believe in you; we praise your Fatherly justice.

Jesus made himself the perfect sacrament of the justice of his Father, making us all blood-brothers and sisters in the covenant which he sealed on the cross. We know that the Father confirmed this new covenant in blood by raising Christ from the dead and giving him a throne at his right hand.

— Lord, we believe in you; we praise your Fatherly justice.

We know that Christ will judge the world according to the new justice. If we have shown concern for the lonely, visited the imprisoned, consoled the oppressed and the depressed, then we shall meet him, the Judge, as our Saviour.

— Lord, we believe in you; we praise your Fatherly justice.

We believe in the Holy Spirit, the giver of all good gifts; we are thus drawn together and can rejoice in the gift of the one Spirit while giving ourselves in the service of our brothers and sisters.

— Lord, we believe in you; we praise your Fatherly justice.

We believe in the one, holy, Catholic and apostolic Church. We are truly a sign of Christ's presence if we hunger and thirst for the justice that makes people believe that we depend on the one Father and are his family.

— Lord, we believe in you; we praise your Fatherly justice.

We profess one baptism, that of Christ, the great manifestation of saving solidarity and we live our baptism if we gather under the cross of Christ and thus around him who is in his glory. We hunger and thirst for justice, that saving justice that frees the prisoners, the addicts and the alcoholics, that heals the sick, restores honour and dignity to all men.

— Lord, we believe in you; we praise your Fatherly justice.

We believe in the communion of saints, the resurrection from the dead, the new heaven and the new earth. This faith is authentic if, now, we hunger and thirst for the hopeful signs of this new earth, of this new heaven, namely, justice and peace among all people.

— Lord, we believe in you; we praise your Fatherly justice.


3. *The social implications*

Of all the beatitudes, the social implications are most evident in this one, where we find Christ looking to the crowd with unlimited thirst and hunger for justice to prevail for the honour of his Father. The basic concept of justice as used in this beatitude and as fully understood when we gather around Christ, transcends the narrow connotation of justice which so frequently is assigned the simple word. Overconcern for the preservation of unjust privileges and the concentration of power in the hands of small groups appear as glaring injustices once we know Christ, the embodiment of that justice newly come from heaven. It is in this light that we must assess the great problems of our day as, for instance, the pro-abortion movement that views doing away with life in a mother's womb as a 'right to privacy'; such a claim rests more often than not on a woman's not wanting to be inconvenienced in her social life. We cannot, however, indulge in the illusion that the life of the unborn child can be protected solely by a state's penal legislation, although we recognize the importance of the laws that remove the causes of abortions, and penal legislation against abortionists who cruelly exploit human weakness. A state vilifies itself if it merely protects the rights of the strong, of the powerful, of those who are vocal. We cannot hope that society will fulfil its social justice in favour of the weakest if there are no personalized social and religious values marked by hunger and thirst for the new justice and a readiness to sacrifice everything with a view to establishing this justice among men. We are truly concerned about the right of the unborn to life and the dignity of each mother when we honour also the unmarried mother, she who at least shows the courage and the fortitude to take upon herself the consequences of her actions, which resulted in the transmission of new life. We do not condone extramarital sexual rapports but we honour those who, in spite of their human frailty, manifest a sense of responsibility for their behaviour. Whoever discriminates against unmarried mothers or against so-called illegitimate children stands accountable for many abortions.

After a public conference on abortion in the United States, I engaged in personal dialogue with a social worker who, during the public discussion, stated that she frequently advised poor people to abort and helped them obtain the abortion. While I was speaking with her in a friendly way, because publicly I had responded too sharply, we were approached by two persons, one of whom was a priest; they gave the lady their address and telephone number saying: 'Whenever, in the future, you find young women whose poverty might be an indication for abortion, call me; I shall assume the responsibility. There should be no reason whatsoever to advise abortion as an easy solution'. This, it seems to me, is the most appropriate sign of a hunger and thirst for saving justice.

Another terrible plague of our society is the growing criminality rate. There are some who seek a solution in the death penalty and other sharp vindictive measures for justice. By no means do I exclude punishment if it can help protect the innocent. But if we believe in Jesus Christ, we shall not consider cruel punishment for those who act cruelly. Rather, we believe in the healing and saving justice of the Saviour. We need to be converted to mutual respect and to a total education oriented towards non-violence, peace and justice, and allow concern for the dignity of each person, that is, commitment to renewed social structures, to serve as the recommended preventive remedy against criminality.

Our prisons degrade people; prisoners who leave after years in our correctional systems are worse than when they entered. Here again we need that hunger and thirst which Christ brought in order to bring about change. Some time ago, I met a group of sisters to whom I had spoken at the time of the Council. With a smile, they asked me where I would place them. I had to make an effort to recollect what we had discussed earlier, namely, that I expected the religious of the future to be present in jails as social workers because of their great healing power. These sisters, and among them was a former superior general, had trained as social workers and, indeed, they are now there where Christ is visited. 'Whoever visited them, has visited me' (Mt 25:36).

The faith which we celebrate in the Eucharist when gathered around Christ who continues to proclaim his beatitudes, is a living and saving faith only if it prompts us to commit ourselves to social justice, to peace among all nations. If the awareness of our union with God is growing, we shall become so conscious of our solidarity that we shall hunger and thirst for justice and find appropriate ways to give witness.

What a pity it would be for someone to think that immediate and effective action for social justice deters people from prayer, from contemplation and evangelization. If we have truly understood that hunger and thirst of Christ for God's justice on earth, we shall surely understand better what constitutes genuine prayer and contemplation. It will energize us to proclaim the

47

good news in such a way that it contains the dynamics of the new justice.

* * *

Lord Jesus Christ, you made visible your hunger and thirst for justice when you prayed for those who crucified you and when you assured the brigand by your side of your everlasting friendship.

You have come to kindle the fire of love and of saving justice. Grant to us, O Lord, that we may so gather around you that we can share your burning desire to see the Father honoured on earth. May we live the life of your most privileged children by going out to those who are most in need of our services.

Lord, liberate us from all selfishness, individual and collective; free the rich and powerful from a narrow conception of justice; set us free from that notion of justice that would have us serve only those who can repay us. Let us rejoice in serving those who come from below and whom you send from above, those who have nothing to offer save their need and their dignity as human beings.

Lord, make us grateful when we celebrate your saving justice. Lord, make us vigilant so that we may discover the many opportunities to make known your justice to all people.

## Chapter 6

## BLESSED ARE THE MERCIFUL;
## MERCY SHALL BE SHOWN TO THEM

### 1. *The merciful Christ*

On the mount of the beatitudes, the disciples gathered around Jesus who is mercy and compassion incarnate. His whole life and death proclaim and radiate this beatitude. Mercy must be seen in the light of the preceding text on God's saving justice. God manifests justice towards his own name as Father by all the revelations of his mercy. The image of God that is revealed in Jesus Christ, the great sacrament of the presence of the Father, is that of God who is at the same time holy and merciful. Following the great prophetic tradition, Mary sings in her life and in the Magnificat: 'His name is holy; his mercy sure from generation to generation towards those who fear him' (Lk 1:49-50).

The image of God projected in the philosophy of Aristotle and in the ethics of the Stoa is that of an immobile God, one who, because of his absolute perfection as prime cause, is unable to be moved by mercy and compassion. Compassion seems to be incompatible with his absolute sovereignty as the prime mover. On the contrary, the revelation of God through the prophets and his final and perfect revelation in Jesus Christ is that of God who, because of his holiness and absolute perfection, is merciful without end. Thus speaks God through the prophet Hosea: 'My people are diseased through their disloyalty and yet, Israel, how could I give you up? My heart recoils from it; my whole being trembles at the thought. I will not let loose my fury, I will not destroy Ephraim again, for I am God, not man: I am the Holy One in your midst and have no wish to destroy' (Hosea 11:7-9).

Jesus Christ round whom we gather not only speaks of the blessedness of mercy, he personifies it as its absolute and final embodiment, the great sacrament of the Father's mercy. Whoever sees Christ knows the compassion of the heavenly Father and whoever, through Jesus Christ, knows the Father and honours him as absolute mercy, knows the way of salvation, that of mercy and compassion as God has shown it through Jesus Christ. The whole life of Jesus, particularly his death, supremely reveals the merciful love of God.

Throughout the gospel we see how wonderfully Jesus receives sinners and restores them to a sense of dignity; note how he deals with the woman of Samaria whom everyone knew to be a sinner. How amazingly he expresses his healing forgiveness of the woman whom the Pharisees had brought to him as an adulteress to be stoned. Jesus manifests the heavenly Father as a compassionate Good Shepherd just as foretold by the prophet Ezekiel: 'For these are the words of the Lord God: Now I myself will ask after my sheep and go in search of them. I am going to look after my flock myself and keep all of it in view. As a shepherd keeps all his flock in view when he stands up in the middle of his gathered sheep, so shall I keep my sheep in view. I shall rescue them from wherever they have been scattered during the dark and cloudy days . . . I myself will show them where to rest. . . . I will search for the lost, recover the straggler, bandage the hurt, strengthen the sick' (Ezek 34:11-16).

Jesus more particularly manifests the mercy of the Father to those who are gathered around him under his cross; they enjoy the fullest possible revelation of the merciful love of God. Jesus not only consoles the pious women, his mother and the beloved disciple; he also prays for those who nailed him to the cross: 'Father, forgive them for they do not know what they are doing' (Lk 23:34). What greater mercy could he have shown to the criminal who was crucified with him than to assure him of his abiding presence: 'In very truth, I tell you, today you shall be with me in Paradise' (Lk 23:43). In his most terrible suffering, he does not revert to self-pity; on the contrary, he opens himself totally to the concerns of others. When he calls Judas 'Friend', there is no sarcasm in the appellation; it is the last merciful attempt to save and to convert the faithless friend. When Peter had three times denied his friendship with Jesus to the point of swearing to not knowing him, Jesus turns to Peter, looks him straight in the eye so that Peter may read the mercy in his own eyes. Thus it is that Jesus proclaims to us in the sermon in the plain as on the mount: 'Be therefore as merciful as your heavenly Father' (Lk 6:36).

When ascending the mount of the beatitudes, Christ invites us to gather under the cross and to gather around him who is the risen Lord. He reminds us that all the splendour of the resurrection is given to him because he has fully revealed the mercy of his heavenly Father.

\* \* \*

Jesus Christ, Son of man and Son of God, we adore you; we praise you; we glorify you in your great mercy. It is in this mercy that the glory of our Father shines through. Let all our voices join with Mary's in singing about your Holy Name for it is because of your name, Son of God, and because of the name of the Father that you show such great mercy to all of us. Lord, make us grateful and merciful.

## 2. Our vocation: to be a living gospel of God's mercy

The one who remains closest to Christ on the mount of the beatitudes as under his cross is Mary. We honour her under the title 'Mother of Mercy'; but we can truly honour and venerate her to the extent that we, too, become a visible image of God's own mercy as revealed in Jesus Christ. Mary is the prototype of the Church who stands as a sacrament of salvation

51

whenever she becomes a visible and attractive sign of the mercy of Jesus Christ and of the heavenly Father. We cannot be faithful to any of God's commandments without faithfulness to his mercy. The real *élites* in the Church reveal, in their lives, the synthesis between fidelity to God's mercy and faithfulness to all of his other commandments.

People frequently speak about their fear of death which is nothing other than fear of the Divine Judge. Yet, we know how to prepare ourselves for a death that will inspire nothing but great trust: it is to live to the fullest the beatitudes; then we know that surely mercy will be shown us. We are justified by pure grace. Salvation is an act of God's merciful justice, but final salvation is also a function of our grateful response to the mercy we have received. The final judgment will be the joyous song of Christ for the blessed who have shown mercy: 'You have my Father's blessing; come, enter and possess the kingdom that has been ready for you since the world was made. For when I was hungry you gave me food; when thirsty, you gave me drink; when I was a stranger, you took me into your home; when naked, you clothed me; when I was ill, you came to my help; when in prison, you visited me' (Mt 25:34-36). Excluded from the heavenly kingdom of the beatitudes will be those who, while having observed all the minutiae of laws and rubrics and casuistry, have shown heartlessness and rigorism towards the needy.

More specially in the celebration of the sacrament of reconciliation are we the disciples who gather around Christ on the mount of the beatitudes. Jesus proclaims his mercy and compassion towards us. He manifests to us his healing forgiveness. But we receive it and are truly healed to the extent that we, too, are transformed and become a living gospel of healing forgiveness.

As we have meditated already, one of the outstanding works of mercy is fraternal correction offered with great gentleness. Today, many think of it as an old-fashioned concept for, they say, 'We are adult and mature people who don't need it'. Yet, St Paul recommends this beatitude to us as one of the outstanding expressions of the 'law of Christ' (Gal 6:2). None of us should be so presumptuous as to think he is never in need of fraternal help. If we must assist others at a critical moment, we are to do it kindly and with the full awareness that there might be moments when we need the same help. We are all part of the pilgrim Church and therefore have to be merciful and respectful towards each other. If we appreciate the good qualities of the other and remind ourselves that the other who is now in trouble may one day be much holier than we are, then we can hope for good results of fraternal correction. It is offered in the right way when we gather together around Christ who continued to proclaim to us the beatitude of the merciful.

\* \* \*

Lord Jesus Christ, we thank you for inviting us to go up the mount with you and be seated next to you so as to perceive better the healing power of your mercy. Open our eyes, O Lord, that we may see the multitude as you see it, that we may learn to show mercy as you have shown mercy to us.

## 3. *The social implications*

The works of mercy have both individual and social dimensions. The Church as a whole and many ecclesial communities are dedicated to the works of bodily and spiritual mercy. Long before states were able to undertake these works, the Church began to build hospitals, to organize the care of the sick, the lepers and so on. The Church likewise feels an obligation to organize assistance programmes for those afflicted by famine, earthquakes or other disasters. The Church would not be able to continue these works unless there were a religious *élite,* that is, people who gather in a special way around Christ to learn from him the blessedness of the works of mercy. Therefore, it is in fidelity to this beatitude that we appeal for vocations to the religious and priestly life, for vocations of the lay people to dedicate themselves to this particular witness of mercy.

If we comprehend the devastating results of the existential vacuum of which Victor Frankl speaks so well, then we realize that pastoral care, the proclamation of the gospel by those who have become a living gospel is one of the acts of mercy most needed in our times.

Every person and each community has its special charism to manifest one of the many aspects of mercy taught by Jesus Christ. He who recognizes the great suffering caused by loneliness will consider the possibility of visiting the old and the lonely, to console them, to pray with them, and to render them modest services. For some people, it is just as important to be listened to, to have someone understand them and assure them of their sympathy as to enjoy their presence. I have come to know a number of senior sisters and other retired people who now find their greatest joy in visiting day after day some lonely and old people; they pray with them, encourage them, allow them to enjoy their presence and attention. When Cardinal Frings, Archbishop of Cologne retired, he asked the new bishop as a favour to be made chaplain of the old priests. Although nearly blind, he daily visited the old and lonely priests; just being with them, he manifested his sympathy and appreciation.

I have often received correspondence from prisoners and, occasionally, from whole groups of them; although it takes some precious time to answer their letters, it has been the most consoling experience to see how appreciative these people are. When all is said and done, we come to realize that they, too, are our brothers and sisters. There are disciples of Christ who regularly visit prisoners who have no family or visitors. I know the wife of a Protestant pastor who, during the last six years, has visited weekly a young negro boy who, since the age of twelve, has been confined almost uninterruptedly within correctional institutions. Through her, he has gained confidence that he will be able to live in freedom, with respect and responsibility towards his fellowmen. This good lady told me recently that she is convinced that this young man will become a great leader. She feels strongly that he was imprisoned because nobody could make use of his extraordinary talents.

We should not be content merely to offer individual assistance although this is very important; we should also unite our energies and talents to bring about a radical reform of the correctional system so that therein the healing forgiveness of Jesus will be made visible. Of course, we need so many people who have a genuine vocation to work within the correctional system as social workers or chaplains.

The German bishops call their concerted action of assistance to the developing nations *Actio Misereor,* that is, the action that expresses Christ's own mercy. Just feeding the hungry cannot suffice but they try to assist the developing nations to cultivate their own talents and resources and so to help themselves. This is one of the best ways of showing mercy. People do not like to be dependent on others forever. These actions should also procure more generous help for the developing nations on the part of our governments. I feel it is a matter of social justice that the wealthy nations who dispose of tremendous material and human resources assist those far less favoured. But whether or not it be justice and mercy for the state, it is certainly a duty of believers to promote a more generous assistance programme for the sake of justice, peace and mercy.

Mercy is not to be misconstrued as permissiveness. A permissive society is merciless; it is the source of degradation, exploitation and despair. Both justice and mercy compel us to guarantee social conditions that permit normal persons to grow to maturity. One of these social conditions is a society in which people can share ideals and accept norms of behaviour which allow people to live happily.

One of the social implications of mercy is an act of amnesty, especially after political conflicts. For me, it is almost unbelievable that after the end of the war in Vietnam, the Nixon government, harassed though it was by the Watergate affair, refused to show any clemency. For the many who decided for conscientious objection because of the senselessness and injustice of the war, it would have been less an act of clemency than one of justice to give amnesty. Others might have had less noble motives when they refused to serve in Vietnam. It is strange, however, that Nixon's successor immediately offered him amnesty even before his case was tried and judged. It is then unintelligible why the government did not decide for general amnesty for those who had refused to serve in the Vietnamese war, whatever their motive. Amnesty is not only an act of clemency but one of reconciliation also. It is within the rights of the Pope, of the episcopates and of other men and women of the Church to continue their appeal for amnesty. It was done in an exemplary fashion by the primate of the Spanish episcopate after the death of Franco. If we believe in God's wonderful clemency, then we shall have to promote similar measures wherever they are helpful for the promotion of peace and reconciliation in our society.

\* \* \*

We praise you, Father, Lord of heaven and earth, for having sent us Jesus Christ to be the great sacrament of your compassionate love for all people. If all our life were to become praise of your mercy and love, our earth would then be transformed into a dwelling of peace and joy.

We come to gather around Jesus Christ, your beloved Son, and to rejoice in his nearness in order to see how merciful he is towards all people. We want to learn from him how to act in the same way.

The mercy you have shown us through your Son is not an empty sentiment, but it is truthfulness of life, especially at the hour of his death. In the name of Jesus, we pray you, Father, to make us sharers of his active mercy and to unite us in his love.

Free us from the dangerous tendencies to act as judges of our fellowmen. You did not send your Son to condemn and judge but to save. If we truly believe and pray in his name, why should we scorn people with troublesome make-ups? Instead, we should meet them with understanding and become an image of Jesus Christ, the Divine Physician, the Good Shepherd. Thus your name will be revealed to the world.

Send us your Holy Spirit so that day by day we can better fulfil the great commandment proclaimed by the life and death of your Son: 'Be therefore merciful as your heavenly Father is merciful'.

Chapter 7

# BLESSED ARE THOSE
# WHOSE HEARTS ARE PURE;
# THEY SHALL SEE GOD

1. *Christ, the embodiment of love and purity*

With the disciples, we are called to go up the mount to meet Christ who has come from heaven to teach us how to love on earth as in heaven; that is, wholeheartedly and with a pure heart.

The whole life of Jesus Christ supremely reveals the holiness of love between the Father and the Son in the Holy Spirit. With the same purity of heart with which Jesus loves the Father he loves the multitude, that is, all his brothers and sisters. Christ is the embodiment, the incarnation of God's pure love. He knows the Father as the One who gave himself completely to his Word, and he loves the Father in the power of the Holy Spirit; that is, in total self-bestowal. His knowledge of the Father is replete with gratitude. By the Holy Spirit, he is consecrated to fulfil the will of the Father in pure love. In all his life, Jesus proclaims that he has not come to do his own will but that of the Father, that he has not come to seek his own glory but that of the Father.

The biblical notion of God's glory comes very close to that of purity of heart. God does not need his creatures; his greatness stands independent of our service. That he takes care of us and manifests himself to us rests solely on the absolute fullness and purity of his love.

Jesus is a perfect mirror-image of that love with which the Father loves him. He is the 'Light of Light', the humble servant who gives himself to those who cannot repay him or who are not at all worthy of his love. He reflects the purity of the love of the Father. In this he is glorified. The eternal glory of the risen Lord's humanity is nothing other than the pure splendour of God's glory.

Christ first loved us with the love of the Father and through the power of the Holy Spirit. It is not we who initiated the love relationship with God. We respond to God's own initiative of first loving us who were devoid of merit. This truth shines through all the words and deeds of Jesus up to his last words on the cross. Therefore, purity of love is one of the most wonderful attributes of God and it is revealed in the name of Jesus.

\* \* \*

Eternal Father, we adore you and praise your glory as it shines forth in the life and death of your beloved Son, Jesus Christ. Let your Holy Spirit come upon us and cleanse us that we may know your name and praise you in your glory for you have loved us only because of your own name, you who are purity and holiness of love.

## 2. *Christ, the source of purity of heart*

Christ shares with us the purity of his love and his zeal for justice when we come to him with a minimum of sincerity and with a longing for greater sincerity in our commitment.

The promise made in this beatitude is wonderful: 'They shall see God'. It means that even here on earth people come to a blissful knowledge of God that is the promise of the ever-lasting beatific vision. God is love and only those who have learned to love in a similar way can have a blissful experience of God and receive that knowledge of God which bears in itself all beatitudes. All the saints and the prophets longed to know God with a pure heart, with all their affection, passions, intellect and will, but they also experienced the impossibility of coming to this kind of experience of God without the purification of heart and mind.

Moses found favour in the presence of God and Yahweh addressed him as one speaks with his friends. So Moses found the courage to ask God the greatest favour: 'You have said, "I know you by name and you have won my favour". If indeed I have won your favour, please show me your countenance, so that I can understand you and win your favour. Remember too that this nation is your own people'. Yahweh replied: 'I will let all my splendour pass in front of you, and I will pronounce before you the name Yahweh. I have compassion on whom I will and I show pity to whom I please. Yet you cannot see my face, for man cannot see me and live'. And Yahweh said: 'Here is a place besides me. You must stand on the rock, and when my glory passes by, I will put you in the crevice of the rock and shield you with my hand while I pass by. Then I will take my hand away and you shall see my back, but you cannot see my face' (Ex 33: 12-23).

The prophet Isaiah had a similar experience of God's purifying and burning holiness; with holy fear, he stood with the Holy God, Lord of the seraphim and cherubim. He cried out: 'What a wretched state I am in. I am lost; for I am a man of unclean lips and live among a people of unclean lips, and yet my eyes have looked at the King, the Lord of Hosts' (Is 6: 5). But then the prophet received the new experience of a purifying fire of God's holiness. One of the seraphs took from the altar a glowing coal with a pair of tongs and touched his mouth and said: 'See now, this has touched your lips; your sin is taken away, your iniquity is purged' (Is 6: 7). Then the prophet rejoiced and he responded with joy to God's calling: 'Here I am, send me' (Is 6: 8).

St John of the Cross concludes, from the teaching of the scriptures, from the whole prophetic and mystic tradition and from his own experiences that even the mystical vision of God as experienced by Moses would cause an immediate death if

E

granted by God to a person who was not yet purified from all free inclination to sin. God is holy love and therefore, like a blissful light for those who are humble and sincere; he is a purifying fire, but for others, this is the cause of the most painful and shocking experience. God gradually reveals himself to his friends, cleansing them more and more from the less than pure motives. If a human person gratefully accepts the purifying fire of God's nearness and converts himself to God with a sincere heart, with profound sorrow for his sins, and puts his trust in God, then he advances more and more in the blissful experience of the beatitude: 'They shall see God'.

It is but a foolish dream for some of today's young people to hope to be able to broaden their capacity for spiritual experience by drugs without the patient effort of conversion to God and their neighbour. The true experience of God can be known only by those who accept the necessary purification from all selfishness and pride. Therefore, we pray with the prophets and the saints: 'Grant to us, O Lord, a heart renewed. Grant to us a new spirit'. If we so pray, it is that we believe conversion to be possible provided we listen to Jesus and stay near him; we then experience his power; he can give us a new heart and a new spirit.

In an ancient manuscript of the gospel of St Luke, the second petition of the Our Father 'Thy kingdom come' gave way to another formulation: 'Let your Holy Spirit come upon us and cleanse us.' Where man's heart is purified so as to be guided by God's gracious love, he makes all his life a grateful and generous response in the service of his fellowmen. There the kingdom of God is at hand. Our prayer for a new heart and a new spirit is sincere when we are at least willing to scrutinize our motives and intentions. The kingdom of God is coming whenever a person seeks God with a sincere heart and joins his fellow men in the sincere search for what is good, truthful and right.

A person with selfish motives living among people having similar ulterior motives will always be blind even if he is knowledgeable about norms, objective principles and all the formulations of Christian dogma. We find the right solution when, in the concrete situations of life, we search for the good together with our fellowmen and stand ready to put into practice what our conscience tells us.

They are blessed people whose heart is pure and who no longer ask slavishly: 'Must I do this under pain of mortal or only under pain of venial sin?' They approach the problem in a totally different way. Guided by the grace of the Holy Spirit, and impelled by pure motives, they will ask: 'How can I render thanks to the Lord for all he has given me? How can I transform all my life into a great thanksgiving worthy of the wonderful generosity with which God has loved me?'

We live on the level of a specifically Christian conscience when we examine all our thoughts, desires, words and deeds in the light of the Eucharist; we then render thanks to the Father for having given us his great gift, Jesus Christ, and we render thanks to Christ who has given himself for us on the cross. If we have learned to adore God in spirit and truth, we shall find the proper criterion for each of our decisions. We shall serve God with a pure heart and decide only for what can be offered God, our Father, as an expression of thanksgiving for all that he has done for us. Our heart will be pure if it is filled with love of God, namely, with the love that Christ revealed to us.

In his recent book on *The Church and the Kingdom of God,* the famous Father Richard Lombardi suggests that all renewal of the Church and all witness to a proclamation of the kingdom of God centre on sincerity of conscience. He frequently refers to this text of the Second Vatican Council found in *The constitution on the Church in the modern world*: 'Conscience is the most secret core and sanctuary of a man. There he is alone with God; his voice echoes in his depths. In a wonderful manner, conscience reveals that law which is fulfilled by love of God and neighbour. In fidelity to conscience, Christians are joined with the rest of men in the search for truth, and for the genuine solution to the numerous problems which arise in the life of individuals and from social relationships. Hence, the more that a correct conscience holds sway, the more persons and groups turn aside from blind choice and strive to be guided by objective norms of morality. Conscience frequently errs from invincible ignorance without losing its dignity. The same cannot be said of a man who cares but little for truth and goodness, or of a conscience which by degrees grows practically sightless as a result of habitual sin' (GS, 16). A sincere conscience that errs is still deplorable but it becomes a moral evil only if the conscience is not sincere or if someone attempts to manipulate the consciences of others. There can be a way of inculcating objective norms, of threatening with sanctions which manifest an impure heart, a moral fanaticism and rigorism that has been a result and a cause of a lack of total commitment to Christ.

\* \* \*

Lord Jesus Christ, we thank you for having come to reveal to us the beatitude of those whose hearts are pure. We are all longing to know you and to know the Father; for this is eternal life. We thank you for having shown us the most fundamental condition for this great blessing. Call us, O Lord, that we may go up with you to the mount and gather around you. You promised us that when you would go up to the Father, you would send us the Holy Spirit. Purity of heart is a gift of your Spirit. Send us the Holy Spirit. Grant to us, O Lord, a heart renewed, a pure heart.

3. *The social implications*

It would be a serious misconception to think of the beatitudes as proclaimed solely for the sake of purity of heart understood just in relation to individual salvation. This beatitude states one of the conditions for eternal beatitude and for personal growth. No other beatitude is as important to our social renewal as this one. A person who knows God and works for his kingdom with pure motives can, with the collaboration of others, live in a more fraternal and more equitable world. What is most lacking in today's world is mutual trust; this cannot be established without absolute sincerity, in our every act or deed, and the purity of our motives.

It is helpful to remember that the first beatitude is the foundation of all the others. Whoever has been converted to Christ, the servant, and has made himself a servant of the common good, of each of our brothers and sisters, will truly work for a better world. On the contrary, he who is always seeking his own convenience, power, career, titles or promotions, will always be tempted to make a very diplomatic use of truths and half-truths, and even distort religious motives in that direction. The prophet Isaiah laments that he has to live with people of impure lips. It is impossible for us to acquire a pure heart and to act with absolutely sincere convictions and motives without co-operating in the creation of a social climate in which sincerity and mutual trust are possible. The disciples of Christ must unite themselves with all men of good will to combat corruption and hypocrisy.

I am thinking especially of Christians called to the noble vocations of educators, journalists, teachers, lawyers, doctors and politicians. If they create a climate of trust and absolute truthfulness, they truly become community builders. They contribute to healthy relationships and so to the health of persons and community. A society is truly civilized, human and redeemed if everyone can trust the sincerity of the words, actions and motives of others, especially of those who exercise authority.

Whoever believes in the kingdom of God and places his trust in the Lord will never think that the cause of religion or that of the common good needs lies and hypocrisy. The Watergate case and the war against corruption prompted by Lockheed and the dealings of other corporations has hopefully opened the eyes of many people. But even this caustic warning serves no useful purpose if we are not truly converted. We cannot create new structures in society without a new way of thinking.

We rejoice that a considerable number of young people today give high priority to sincerity of words and actions as well as to honesty of purpose. It is a gift of the Lord of history if we begin asking ourselves whether or not our motives are upright and examine our words and actions in terms of communicating truthfulness.

Purity of intention, absolute candour and sincerity in communications, is indispensable for those who have dedicated their lives to the service of the gospel and to the fostering of human dignity. It seems to me a form of unbelief for someone to want to help the cause of religion by half-lies. One cannot be a witness to the eternal truth of God's loving and saving presence if one has not purified one's motives and has not learned to communicate in absolute sincerity and trustworthiness. Among the seven injunctions that follow immediately the proclamation of the beatitudes, one of the seven solemn words is a most urgent call to absolute sincerity. 'Again, you have learned that our forefathers were told, "Do not break your oath", and "Oaths sworn to the Lord must be kept". . . . But what I tell you is this: plain "Yes" or "No" is all you need to say; anything beyond that comes from the devil' (Mt 5:33-37). A simple 'yes' or a plain 'no' of a true disciple of Christ finds greater trust than all the oaths of people lacking in sincerity.

In a Church plagued by distrust, we professors of theology had to swear the anti-modernism oath once or twice annually. For this to be understood, one need only consider the negative impact of the Constantinian era where the spirit of careerism, promises of promotions and threats of discrimination greatly undermined sincerity and trustworthiness. We can hope that a transition from the Constantinian era to a faith of personal choice and a Church that cannot remunerate with honours on this earth will help us to understand better the demands of the sermon on the mount.

A certain type of moralism thought only of chastity when the expression 'pure in heart' was mentioned. Of course, chastity also belongs to purity, but only if all human relationships are marked by mutual respect and sincerity can sexuality follow the same rule. There will then be no untrue offers of love and no manipulation of others. Rigid moral norms and heavy threats of mortal sin cannot obtain what absolute sincerity and vigilance over our motives can.

The great experts of brainwashing, Pavlov and Skinner, state plainly that people can and should be completely manipulated through a conditioning process based on fear of sanction and hope of remuneration. Indeed, I am convinced that people who never transcend the immediate incentives of remuneration or operate from fear of punishment are defenceless objects of all kinds of manipulation. He who in his words and actions is seeking only praise, promotion and success is in a hopeless condition as a manipulated manipulator, and he will never make progress in true freedom or in the knowledge of a loving God. Salt for the earth and light for the world are the promoters of true freedom, especially those who are motivated by gratitude towards God, and therefore give a generous response to the needs of others where no reward can be expected.

\* \* \*

God our Father, everyone around us speaks of freedom, boasts of his freedom or cries for freedom. Yet, frequently, the same people who promise freedom are frightful manipulators or have been manipulated to think they have made their own choices. We thank you, Father, for having taught us by your Son Jesus Christ how to set out for true liberation. By loving you with all our heart and learning from your servant, our Lord Jesus Christ, how to serve our brothers and sisters selflessly we shall know you and find the way of true liberty. Give us perseverance, Lord, so that we may go up the mountain with Jesus to listen to his words, treasure them up and learn from him who is absolute purity of love, of justice and of peace.

Chapter 8

# BLESSED ARE THE PEACEMAKERS; GOD SHALL CALL THEM HIS CHILDREN

## 1. *Christ, the Prince of Peace*

Around Jesus we gather in faith and acknowledge him as the Son of God, unique in his dignity. He is recognized by the Father as Son while he makes himself the servant of all. His disciples are deeply touched when they hear him exultantly cry out: 'Abba, Father!' Jesus, Son of the eternal Father, is in no need of claiming the right to call God Father. From the very beginning of his earthly existence the human nature of Christ is united with the eternal Word, and God the Father calls him his Son.

Yet, Jesus manifests himself as the Messiah and the Son of God by making known to everyone that he is the great peacemaker, the Prince of Peace. So is he promised by the prophet: 'For there is a child born for us, a Son given to us to bear the symbol of dominion on his shoulder; and this is the name they give him: Prince of Peace. Wide is his dominion in a peace that has no end' (Is 9: 5-7). Jesus' earthly introduction by the angels is to the sound of: 'Glory to God in the highest heaven and on earth his peace to men of good will' (Lk 2: 14). Jesus not only speaks cogently about peace; he himself is the source, and he shares the gift and mission of peace with his disciples by the power of the Holy Spirit. He is sent to establish peace on earth, the messianic peace:

67

salvation and liberation. There is no other word in the Old Testament that is so full of promise as the word *shalom*, 'peace'. *Shalom* includes all the promises of the messianic age. We can never forget that Jesus, in order to grant us this peace, paid the highest price in his own blood. The blood of the new and everlasting covenant makes us all brothers and sisters in Jesus Christ, eternal Son of the Father.

How great must have been the inner peace of Jesus Christ, for, on the cross, he could turn his eyes to those who crucified him and pray: 'Father, forgive them'. By his peace, he changed the heart of the brigand who was crucified alongside him and assured him of that everlasting peace which is the harvest of his suffering. He is so filled with peace that he always radiates it and shares it, even under trying circumstances where he could have been angry, desolate and frustrated.

The risen Lord greeted his disciples with this wonderful word: '*Shalom*', and at once, they were filled with joy. They not only received forgiveness and the good news about peace; in faith, they received him who is Peace; by opening their heart to this Peace, they recognized and honoured him as the Son of God. Thus they received the mission to proclaim peace, to be witnesses and ministers of an all-embracing reconciliation.

\* \* \*

Jesus Christ, we adore you; we glorify you as Prince of Peace. The Father gave you a name that is above all names. When our heart is filled with your peace, then we know what it means to believe in you, the true Son of God and the Brother of all men. Then we know also what it means to be called children of God.

Send forth your Spirit that, baptized in him, we may come to know you better, our Peace and Reconciliation. Let us be so united in your name and gathered around you that we shall receive your peace more and more gratefully, with the wonderful mission of being messengers of peace. If we are alone with our selfish selves, we can only be disturbed and disturbing to others. But if we follow you on to the mount of the beatitudes, then we receive your peace as a mission to the crowds forever present to your heart, whether it be on the mount of the beatitudes, on Mount Calvary or in your heavenly kingdom.

## 2. Peacemakers with Christ

When we go up the mountain with Christ, it is to receive from him reconciliation and peace. It is by the experience of peace coming from Christ that we come to know how precious a good it is. But we are worthy to be called sons and daughters of God only if we accept this gift with intense gratitude; it subsequently becomes a mission for us to be transformed into peacemakers. Just because the messianic peace is an undeserved gift of the Father in Jesus Christ, the Prince of Peace, and since this gift is destined for all men, we can receive it and abide in it only if we are willing to look to the crowd and serve it as artisans of peace.

If in faith we truly understand this unprecendented honour of being called sons and daughters of the holy God, then we shall pray with all our heart as did St Francis: 'Lord, make me a channel of your peace'. If this prayer is sincere, it will include all the conditions for being an agent of peace. Readiness to serve with Christ, the servant, sorrow for our sins and compassion for people troubled by terrorism and gunfight, all call for a spirit of gentleness and non-violence, a pure heart that desires nothing save helping people to find peace and justice. Whoever receives the peace of God with faith and joy and gratitude becomes, in union with Christ, a source of peace. The more we rejoice in peace and abide with Christ, the Prince of Peace, the greater is our appreciation of our mission to share this peace with all men at all costs.

We should always be mindful of our mission to bring peace to all the people we meet, not forgetting that we cannot share with others what we do not possess; we have to maintain peace of heart and mind in order to proclaim it effectively. What an absurdity to lose one's peace of mind because of petty inconveniences. Even if the annoyance is considerable, there is no proportion with the gift of peace.

Immediately after a workshop on the sacrament of peace and our mission to be peacemakers, a good priest brought me to the airport. He had confirmed and re-confirmed my flight reservations to be absolutely sure that nothing would go wrong. But when we arrived at the airport — we did arrive on time — we were told that because of certain schedule changes, there would be no seat for me on that flight. My dear friend exploded with indignation and wrath; he even used acrimonious expressions. I interrupted him and said: 'But my dear friend, did we not celebrate, for a whole week, the joy of the Lord and our mission to be peacemakers? How is it possible for you to get so angry?' His response was: 'It is already lost; of course, I know it is absurd, but I have truly lost all joy and peace'. Is this not a frequent occurrence among too many of our friends and possibly ourselves? I think we could forestall these explosions, fits of anger and sadness if we were only more aware of the presence of Christ who is our Peace; more thought can be given to the greatness of his gift and the honour that is ours to be children of God if we are peacemakers.

*Shalom*, peace: it is God's gift and a gift of stupendous totality. Peace and reconciliation mean new relationships: a new relationship with God our Father, with Christ, our Lord and Brother, with our neighbour as seen in Jesus Christ, with the whole world around us and last, but not least, with ourselves. Knowing that God accepts us as we are, we too can accept our burden and can even bear a part of the burden of our fellowman. Messianic peace tells us that we are accepted by God as his children. God himself comes to meet us where we are in order to lead us to the fullness of our dignity as his children. We therefore see our whole life in a new light: we view the shadows and the difficulties of our own character, the shadows and the tensions in the world around us. The whole comes to be seen in time in a totally new light and in fresh perspectives with the firm hope that we shall grow to the fullest stature of the sons and daughters of God. We must realize that this is what is meant by being accepted by God; we shall then be able to love our neighbour as he is and to invite him to walk along with us on the road to peace, to fullness in Christ.

If we are aware that we are gathered around Christ on the mount of the beatitudes, we shall then remember how he received Mary Magdalen, the woman of Samaria, Peter who had denied him, and how he allowed these people to put all their trust in him. He made them new persons through the gifts of his peace, especially the gift of courage, through which he will enable us also to deepen the peace in ourselves and to be totally dedicated to the mission of peacemakers.

\* \* \*

Lord Jesus Christ, how terrible it would be to doubt constantly whether or not we are forgiven. We thank you for having come with healing forgiveness as the reconciler, as our peace. We thank you for your words and your sacrament that assure us of this peace. We equally thank you for giving us the great honour of being with you forsterers of peace and reconciliation among people.

We pray with St Francis: 'Lord, make me an instrument of your peace. Where there is hatred, let me sow love; where there is injury, pardon; where there is doubt, faith; where there is despair, hope; where there is darkness, light; and where there is sadness, joy. O Divine Master, grant that I may not so much seek to be consoled as to console; to be understood as to understand; to be loved as to love; for it is in giving that we receive; it is in pardoning that we are pardoned; and it is in dying that we are born to eternal life'.

## 3. The social implications

It is fitting to underline the personal aspect of the peace Christ grants us, peace of heart and mind; that is, a new relationship with God which paves the way for a greater acceptance of ourselves. However, we must not forget for one moment the social, all embracing reality of the peace which

Christ himself has given and for which he makes us his instruments and ambassadors. Christ came for the reconciliation of all peoples among themselves, and with the Father. We cannot honour Christ as Prince of Peace unless we foster peace to the best of our ability, on all levels, in the economic, social, political, national and international realms.

A certain verticalism frequently forgot that the peace of Christ is an indivisible entity. We cannot deepen our peace of mind without accepting peace in its wholeness, in all its dimensions. It is not possible to seize only a piece of it. Whoever opens himself with gratitude to this gift of the Lord will also accept the fullness of the mission. Whoever truly desires peace of mind and his share in the peace of the new heaven and new earth will commit himself to peace among people in both the private and the social spheres.

I am thinking primarily of peace in the family. It is possible to live the sacrament of marriage, to become truly signs of God's presence for each other; the husband and wife then respect each other, love each other and are thus ready to ask for and to grant forgiveness graciously. Whoever believes in Christ's peace will not impose humiliating conditions on others or even ask for unconditional surrender.

Christians who have accepted from the risen Lord the mission of being messengers of peace will never be fanatics or rigorists. The Pharisees, because of their legalism, were unable to open themselves to the peace of Christ just as they were unable to become messengers of his peace.

Jesus meets us where we are and accepts us as his companions on the road provided only that we are willing to move in the right direction. In a similar way, we are to accept each other in our communities and patiently, kindly help each other on the road to the fullness of peace.

Messianic peace includes, of necessity, social justice and peace. Whoever truly wants to gather around Christ, the Prince of Peace, will never allow himself to promote or defend unjust economic, social or political positions. We shall not vote for representatives whose unjust political leanings are known. Those who are messengers of peace and agents of reconciliation will fight constantly against individual and collective egotism.

In recent years, I have frequently met with refugees from Burundi who, in extreme danger of their life, escaped from terrible massacres. About 250,000 members of the tribe of the Hutus were killed. The Hutus are a majority of about eighty to eighty five per cent of the population, and the Tutsi, a minority of about twelve per cent, have traditionally exploited the Hutus and refused them any share in decision-making. The massacre eliminated almost all those who, education-wise, would have been qualified for positions of leadership and so to participate in the government. The situation does not leave much hope for a peaceful reconciliation and yet the vicious cycle of revenge looks even darker.

In one of these meetings with a group of qualified refugees, we prayed and I think all came to understand the great gift of reconciliation and of peace that comes from God, that enables us to hope against all appearances to the contrary. The programme presents itself as 'justice without revenge; peace in justice and pardon'. These intelligent refugees decided to be most careful not to generalize that all the members of the minority tribe of Tutsi are responsible for the massacre. On the contrary, acts by which Tutsis saved members of the Hutu tribe should be brought to the foreground. It is a matter of freeing the dominant Tutsi class from fear, because the anxiety of the besieged minority again and again produces violence and oppression.

It seems to me fundamentally important that all who accept the special mission of peacemakers make clear their purpose to commit themselves to justice, excluding any thought of revenge. There must be a firm opposition to any collective egotism that offers an unjust peace to those who submit unconditionally or renounce their most basic rights.

Christ did not come to ratify an unfair or false peace. On the contrary, he has mercilessly unmasked the lies of the unjust about peace. Neither does Christ allow inertia. Whoever wants to witness to Christ, the Prince of Peace, must pool his energies with those of all men of good will. Those are persons qualified to make known Christ as Peace who combine the spirit of gentleness with the hunger and thirst for justice, but a justice that forgives and heals wounds.

The society of today and probably that of the next decade must fight a hard battle against organized crime, fanatic extremists who use all kinds of violence and terrorism against their fellow-countrymen, especially those called to protect the public order. We surely need a trained police force and we give due respect to these men who defend the lives of the innocent. However, to think that strong police forces and the death penalty are sufficient to resolve the problem is erroneous and ludicrous. Along with the commitment of good people to the creation of an atmosphere of respect for each human person, we need the intelligence of all with a view to removing the main causes of criminality and terrorism. The world needs the disciples of Christ who have learned from him to be gentle while firmly committed to justice. There is a need for radical conversion.

The concerns of Christians cannot be limited to their own tribe or to their own nation. As one who renders thanks to Christ, the peacemaker will have an impassioned interest in peace among all nations. In order to promote a policy of *détente*, of dialogue and of generous help for developing nations, one needs to know more about the situations we confront. This new understanding of our all-embracing mission is probably most characteristic of the group of American nuns called *The Network*. They dedicate themselves to the difficult task of becoming informed about key social issues and their relation to politics. At present, they have set for themselves the goal of conscience-rousing among politicians.

We are all in the same boat and, if it sinks, we are all part of the catastrophe. We have no right to hope for salvation and peace without committing ourselves strongly to the cause through united efforts. Such is the design of God revealed in Jesus Christ. He wants us to be co-workers of peace and co-revealers of his saving justice.

The progress of peace and reconciliation depends on an enlightened and sane public opinion. Many political decisions depend on the quality of the prevailing public opinion. Therefore, a good part of our energies must be dedicated to this field. We are never allowed to speak contemptuously of the other side; on the contrary, we should always express our appreciation and highest respect for those who think differently from us. Our next-door neighbour, members of our community, because of different educational backgrounds and different temperaments, cannot always be in agreement with us. We must learn the art of disagreeing without being disagreeable. We can never allow ourselves to generalize judgments of groupings within the Church, our society or other nations. Our opposition to Marxism does not allow us to bicker or to vote against the Communist Party candidate just because 'communists are villains'. Frequently, and especially in Italy but also in other countries, they are not atheists and do not truly adhere to the Marxist ideology. People occasionally vote for the Communist Party in order to express their protest against the injustice of the party in power. They bring their discontent to the polls and oppose the behaviour of those who call themselves Christians in politics. And if we know the people to be truly atheists, we should examine ourselves and the attitudes of our group as to whether or not we are responsible for their reaction against inappropriate and sometimes anachronistic religious teachings or practices. We should at least ask ourselves whether we are convincing witnesses.

We are never allowed to speak with contempt of the Russian people merely because they are dominated and oppressed by the Communist Party. I am convinced of the goodness of the great majority of Russian people who desire peace, freedom and justice. Over-generalizing negative judgments are not only a sin against truth and justice but also against our mission as peacemakers. A careful and respectful way of expressing our disagreement, coupled with a sober distinction between ideology and the people involved, would help create favourable conditions for social and political reconciliation.

The manner in which we deal with our polarization in religious communities and within the Church is of great relevance to our peace mission in a secular society. It is inevitable, in a time of cultural upheaval and Church renewal, that there

F

should be tensions and polarizations. Christians are a part of their culture and their era. We can accept diversity of opinion in our religious communities or parishes, in our dioceses, in our Church, while at the same time respecting each other, continuing a fruitful dialogue in readiness to listen, to learn and to unlearn. We can express our convictions in a gentle and humble way; for then we already contribute to the kind of dialogue that is necessary in our secular society. Whenever we have good reasons to be uncertain about our own opinions and hesistant about our options, it would be much better to propose them as questions instead of theses. A patient dialogue never, however, allows a delay for urgent actions needed for social justice, or for national and international peace.

The Eucharistic celebration unites people of the most diverse cultural, economic and social backgrounds. If we accept each other and truly gather around Christ, Prince of Peace, who is also the embodiment of hunger and thirst for justice, the community of faith will surely have its impact on economic, cultural, social, political and international life.

Great is the honour and joy of being called sons and daughters of God and of being urgently invited by Jesus to follow him in his mission of peace on earth. This honour and joy is surely one of the greatest forces and it can have a great impact on the future of society. The mission for peace and justice, a justice in peace, is not a task imposed from without. For anyone who truly believes in the gospel, it arises from within. Pope Paul has frequently appealed to all men to commit themselves to peace and justice, and he offers as motive for the good news: 'Peace is possible'. Whoever believes in Jesus Christ who is Peace Incarnate believes in the possibility that much can be done for peace among nations; if it is possible, then we cannot excuse laziness or pessimism.

\*　\*　\*

Jesus Christ, our Lord and our Brother, you revealed the Father to us in your zeal to unite all peoples in peace and thus reveal that they are all children of the same Father and akin to each other. Send us your Spirit so that our life may bear fruit in love, joy and peace. Make us grateful for the great gift of peace you have brought, so that we can readily accept the sometimes difficult task of being apostles and servants of reconciliation and peace. Never allow us to forget the price you paid, so that we too shall be ready to pay whatever price is necessary when peace is at stake.

Forgive us our sins of envy and of jealousy and all sins against the honour and dignity of our brothers and sisters or whatever has diminished fraternal harmony. Make us aware of the source of many of these sins; is it that we have failed to go up the mount of the beatitudes with you? Even if we did meditate and pray, did we forget that you came for the multitude?

Help us to preserve peace in all the situations of life; grant us peace of mind and the joy of the gospel so that, with you and through you, we can radiate peace, goodness, benevolence, kindness and gentleness to those around us.

Chapter 9

# BLESSED ARE THOSE
# WHO HAVE SUFFERED PERSECTION
# FOR THE CAUSE OF RIGHT;
# THE KINGDOM OF HEAVEN IS THEIRS

1. *Christ, the embodiment of the heavenly kingdom*

It is not by chance that the eighth beatitude concludes with
the same promise as the first: 'The kingdom of heaven is
theirs'. Christ in person is the embodiment of the kingdom of
heaven. He did not come to seek his own glory. He rejects
very energetically the temptation coming from the expectations
of his relatives and his people, who seek a power-messiah and
look forward to Israel's being a superpower. Christ came as
the servant of all people and so is servant of Yahweh. He
suffered for rightness, that is, for the all-embracing justice of
the heavenly Father who wants to unite all nations in justice
and peace.

The morality of the beatitudes is that of the paschal
mystery. Therefore, there is nothing more urgent for us than
to follow Christ to Mount Calvary and then to the mount of
the beatitudes. We come together around Christ who died for
us, has risen for us, wants to continue his mission through the
credible proclamation of the beatitudes and through disciples

who believe that they can live the gospel, and want to live it, regardless of price. Christ himself is the Blessed One in our midst; he is persecuted because of his hunger and thirst for the new justice. He is the Prophet who brings the entire history of the prophets to its culmination. He rouses the conscience of the rich and powerful, of the privileged classes, especially of the religious hypocrites who abuse religion by having pious works and practices, as well as man-made religious traditions, serve their own individual and collective egotism.

If Christ had restricted his ministry to exhortations for personal peace of mind without addressing himself to the burning problems of life in community, of social justice, of absolute sincerity in all human relationships, he would have failed to unmask the great abuse and alienation found in organized religion. Besides, he would not have been persecuted by the political and religious leaders of his time.

Christ mobilized all energies in view of uniting all men in the kingdom of justice and peace which he brings from the Father. He committed himself to the proclamation of the gospel, stirring in people that faith which visibly manifests our belief in one God, Creator and Father of all. Since man was enslaved in collective sinfulness, he had to use forcible and forthright speech to open the eyes of the blind leaders and to succour the misled people. He expresses potent truth for the potentates of this earth. He did not steer clear of confrontations with wealthy and powerful people of obstinate and hypocritical conscience. He smites those hypocrites who employ pious words and appeal to man-made traditions in the name of God with the sole intention of preserving their superiority while placating their critics. Jesus criticizes because he is evidently interested in religion as community under religious leaders.

Jesus Christ is not simply a prophet but the Prophet in whom the great prophetic tradition of Israel finds its culmination as well as its final conflict with the priestly class. All the prophets are characterized by that hunger and thirst for justice that is anchored in their faith in one God. Christ is the perfect monotheist who lives in relationship with the One God and Father of all men in such a way that he challenges all who

80

give lip-service to monotheism but fail to include, in their love and reverence, all of God's creatures. The uncompromising leaders of Jewish organized religion did not open themselves to his message and to his prophetic protest, and so they decided to do away with him. He paid an even higher price than all other prophets before him for his prophetic vocation. He clearly indicates to his disciples that those who receive the charism of prophet will have to follow him.

The fact that this beatitude is proclaimed by the Prophet addressing all who share his vocation and mission sheds a totally new light on the concept of original sin. In the teaching of Jesus, there is little emphasis on the age-old first Adam who committed the first sin by refusing to do the good he could have done and yielding to the evil he could have avoided. The sinful world pivots on closed-mindedness, collective arrogance and abuse of religion. The history of the sin of the world is expressed mainly in the killing of the prophets and, subsequently, in the repudiation of Jesus Christ by the religious leaders of Israel and the masses they had seduced. This sinfulness of the world continues in blindness to the signs of the times and in the persecution of those who have accepted the challenge of the signs of the times and exhibit the courage to appeal to the crowds, especially to the political and religious leaders, for openness to the present opportunities.

Jesus Christ, who bears the burden of all, demonstrates saving solidarity in his prophetic protest and suffering whereby he unmasks the solidarity of perdition marked by blindness and alienation. The kingdom proclaimed by the humble servant, a kingdom of peace, of justice and of mutual trust and respect, is opposed to lust for power, to hypocrisy, to lack of sincerity and abuse of authority.

Centuries before the coming of Christ, Plato wrote: 'If the perfect and just man would appear, the evil people would crucify him'. Christ is the just, the Holy One sent from heaven. His very holiness is the strongest challenge to those imprisoned in their self-righteousness and arrogance. It is the most forceful appeal to conversion, to commit ourselves to justice if we are to follow him. Those who find themselves in a favourable position and yet refuse to accept Christ and his challenge will inevitably join those who are persecuting him.

* * *

Lord Jesus Christ, your words and your death are a provocative challenge to me. I want to accept it because it is the good news that we can be converted to absolute sincerity, to a faith that will never manipulate others. We adore you as the perfect embodiment of the kingdom of the Father. We praise you as the Prophet and as the One who has made visible to us the meaning of faith in one God, and Father.

Lord Jesus Christ, keep us from the great temptation of making you a private and sweet Jesus who would have nothing to do save consoling our souls. Protect our religious leaders from the temptation of preaching conversion to others while they remain unwilling to commit themselves thoroughly to renewal of the Church and the call for justice in the world.

## 2. Gathered around Christ, the Prophet

Whoever in faith has truly met Jesus, the Prophet, constantly with him turns his and our attention to the multitude. He does not allow favouritism for privileged religious or social groups who would think only of themselves and the protection of their interests.

If we are truly gathered around Christ and strengthen each other in our faith, we shall not lose our inner peace because of misunderstanding and defamation. We know all too well the victory of Christ who came to establish justice and peace on earth; he lived as the saving conflict. If Christ died for us, accepting the suffering that came from the self-righteous, the hypocrite, the blind and the arrogant, we then find it normal that the most zealous disciples of Christ will have to cope with similar experiences. Whoever wholeheartedly accepts the vocation to be holy is merciful, compassionate as the heavenly Father, and hungers and thirsts for justice as did Jesus; he will have to suffer opposition even in religious communities and from many influential people in the Church. Of necessity, he will be opposed by those who remain unwilling to accept the gospel in its main dimensions and purposes.

Those who love the Church of Christ will sometimes be faced with the unpleasant duty of protesting against those attitudes and deeds from persons in authority who have not kept themselves open to the joys and hopes, the needs and the anguishes of the people. In the Church founded by Christ, the Prophet, there is no room for blind obedience and slavish submission. In the midst of the great turmoil in Portugal, one bishop dared utter these words: 'A Catholic will always be obedient to his bishop even if he is erring; for it is an honour to err with the Church'. Of course, we must not generalize and state that he is representative of today's bishops. However, if a bishop who has slavishly served an authoritarian regime now requests blind obedience, and so claims identification with the Church, he must be contradicted in the name of Jesus. If a bishop holds such an unevangelical position, then it is not the Church that errs; the Church is then on the side of those who, in the name of Jesus, the Prophet, protest even when they have to suffer and stand as objects of discrimination from men in the system. The Church would have fulfilled her role better in the world if, in times of corruption and infidelity, there had been more prophetic courage and more endurance on the part of believers. Whenever anyone thinks that he has a prophetic mission in the Church or in society, he should question himself as to whether he can truly carry it out for the Church or for society by a readiness to bear the burden of such a vocation; is he ready to suffer without allowing himself to become bitter and angry? One who protests in the name of Jesus and has to suffer must also allow others discernment as to whether or not he is bearing the fruits of the Spirit: joy, peace, kindness, benevolence, goodness, gentleness, self-control.

In the critical times of the Reformation and anti-Reformation, Erasmus of Rotterdam was probably the most learned man alive. Martin Luther and Melanchthon were firmly convinced that the intellectual *élite* would be on their side if they succeeded

G

in winning over Erasmus to their cause. However, he remained in the Church whose failures, abuses and shortcomings he was more aware of than any of his contemporaries. It was because of his trust in God and his hope that a reform of the Church was possible that he had the courage to protest, to speak out with prophetic frankness. Perhaps one of the most desperate efforts of this man to call the responsible leaders of the Catholic Church to renewal in thinking, teaching and living was his book, *Morias Encomion,* that is, *In Praise of Foolishness.* It begins with the words: 'Coming from Italy, I have no energy to dedicate myself to serious work but neither can I indulge in laziness'. He was so appalled by the unwillingness of the Roman Curia to listen to the challenging voices from the reformers outside the Church and from the saints within the Church that he expressed himself in a book dedicated to his holy friend, Thomas More; he used expressions that were appropriately reserved to clowns. He ridiculed the men of the Church who made a show of their high titles, coloured vestments and ignorance. He countered those who were angry with his 'Praise of foolishness' by pointing out how their reaction was an indication of their bad conscience and security complex. One can question whether all the words of Erasmus were pondered either against the background of evangelical mildness or that of Christ's unique frankness when dealing with degenerate religious leaders. There is no doubt, however, that from time to time, organized religion needs men as faithfully dedicated as Erasmus, as learned while at the same time as concerned and courageous in their expression of prophetic discontent.

People unwilling to listen to the strong voices of prophets try to single out their weaknesses and may even invent some. Such was the case against Erasmus of Rotterdam as against Martin Luther King. None of the prophets came close to the holiness of Christ although he found the greatest opposition. There were enemies who wanted to defame him and so concocted all kinds of lies. It is true, however, that fragile men and women with a prophetic charism are aware of their own weaknesses; they realize that in the fulfilment of their vocation, they are vulnerable. Their imperfections give rise to misunderstanding which adds to their suffering. But this can also enter into proper perspective with the beatitudes; contention can lead the prophets to be even more generous, humble and unselfish in fulfilling their mission. It happens that we have to suffer while seeking nothing other than the best for our community, for the Church and society, hence, the glory of God. Bearing in mind our past sins and shortcomings will keep us from being overwhelmed by contradiction, especially when we are most faithful to our vocation. I am not saying either that we have to suffer only for others. Suffering for God's kingdom serves also as reparation for our sins.

Jesus personally speaks forthrightly to his disciples, and indeed, to all of us about our mission to share in the paschal mystery by suffering persecution: 'How blessed you are, when you suffer insults and persecution and every calumny for my sake. Accept it with gladness and exultation, for you have a rich reward in heaven; in the same way they persecuted the prophets before you' (Mt 5:11-12). The immediacy and challenge in Jesus' address personalize his message of the eighth beatitude but apply to all of them. Each of us is intended and called by name, and all are able to respond if gathered together around Christ. Jesus grants us that with the gracious assistance of his Spirit and inspired by the gospel, we can find that inner peace that makes us exult in the midst of suffering. Such serenity is possible if we are filled with faith in the paschal mystery.

Christ is not a philosopher who systematically discourses in abstract terms. He shares with us his own mystery. His words become a law written in our hearts through the celebration of the paschal mystery, through faith, through trust, according to the promptings of the Holy Spirit. If Christ abides in us and we in him, then the great faith of St Francis will also be ours: 'We can live the gospel, we want to live it, and of course, we must live it'. We can live with Christ, the gentle and humble servant, with him who is the embodiment of God's mercy, with him who hungers and thirsts for justice while he is committed to the work of peace, and even when he has to bear the cross of all of us. If we are truly committed to the gospel proclaimed on the mount of the beatitudes, and on Mount Calvary, and inscribed in our hearts by the risen Lord, then we become more aware that we have to pay the price as the prophets did, but this awareness will not be a cause of dangerous frustration so long as we put our trust in the Lord. As long as we believe that suffering for the heavenly kingdom in the service of our fellowmen is a part and parcel of our friendship with Jesus, we are on the way to final peace. We can rejoice in peace, abound in hope if not dance for joy considering all that the Lord has already granted us and promised us. Freed from the useless frustrations that come from personal selfishness and egotism, we can face the difficulties and battles that are inevitable for those who hunger and thirst for justice and dare to unmask hypocrisy even in religious people. We will do so humbly and patiently because of the solidarity binding us to Christ and also because, repeatedly, we discover in ourselves the hidden atheist, the temptation to half-truths and possibly even to pharisaical hypocrisy.

In a critical moment, Peter did disown Jesus when he came to the realization that Jesus had not come to build Israel as a civil power. And yet, Peter was not abandoned by Jesus; once he had received the power from above he looked for suffering in the fellowship of Christ in a new way: 'My dear friends, do not be bewildered by the fiery ordeal that is upon you, as though it were something extraordinary. It gives you a share in Christ's suffering, and that is cause for joy; and when his glory is revealed, your joy will be triumphant. If Christ's name is flung in your teeth as an insult, count yourselves happy because then that glorious Spirit which is the Spirit of God is resting upon you. If you suffer, it must not be for murder, theft, or sorcery, nor for infringing the rights of others. But if anyone suffers as a Christian, he should feel it no disgrace, but confess that name to the honour of God' (1 Pet 4: 12-16).

* * *

Lord Jesus Christ, we thank you for having invited us to join you on the mount of the beatitudes, and in the joyous celebrations of the paschal mystery, in the deep experience of your peace. Grant to us that inner fortitude that allows us to be witnesses of your suffering and of the hope promised to us when we are put to the test. Let us never forget that we cannot follow you to the mount of the beatitudes if we refuse your invitation to follow you on the way to Calvary and to be gathered under your cross. Send us your Spirit and fill us with that glad and grateful faith which is our strength in the midst of turmoil and opposition.

## 3. *The social implications*

The social implications of the activity, witness and suffering of the prophets and their disciples are most obvious. The promise that those who suffer for the cause of right will share the heavenly kingdom also opens on to this social horizon. To belong to the heavenly kingdom means to be guided by God's gifts, to be gathered to work for unity so that it becomes evident that, together, we acknowledge the all-embracing kingdom of God and of his messenger, Jesus Christ. Whoever truly believes in the encompassing lordship of God will do his best to make this visible and effective in the Church and in his family, as in economic, cultural and political life.

Political theology has shown that all religious attitudes and decisions have their impact on the life of society. The same applies to an individualistic approach to religion which fails to activate the yeast of the gospel; instead, it introduces an individualistic tendency in all realms of life. An overemphasis on obedience and conformity, and the one-sided priestly tradition in periods of Church history have proved damaging both for the Church and for society. Whenever the life of the Church reflects Christ, the Prophet, and wherever there are numbers of people ready to follow him and to suffer for the cause of right, there the Church remains the salt of the earth.

We should not narrowly restrict activity for the cause of right as having a social bearing only when it is successful. As Christians, we believe in the social fecundity of suffering. Christ redeemed us on the cross; there he paved for us the way to a better world and he showed us the power of unselfish love. The suffering of the apostles and of all those committed to justice and peace completes, in the life of the disciples, the paschal mystery. Surely, nothing is lacking in the suffering of Christ as such, but it is the design of God that the mission of Christ, including his suffering, should be carried on throughout history by his disciples.

Mahatma Gandhi and Martin Luther King, inspired by the gospel, have enriched the world by their activity, by their witness, by their power to convince and to gather others. But they have also given us an eloquent witness by their death. They have sealed their mission by their blood. The history of the Church gives us many examples of prophetic men and women who have suffered; they were temporarily discriminated against and sometimes excommunicated. The Church venerates a good number of saints who, during their lifetime, had suffered greatly under a Church authority that failed to respond to the prophetic message of the saint. Many others are not canonized; yet, they are recognized by a great part of Christianity as pioneers. Cardinal Newman, Rosmini and so many others have given a radiant witness of their fidelity to the gospel and loyalty to the Church in the midst of machinations and oppositions.

Whoever believes in Christ, the Redeemer of the world, and in the kingdom of the Father which he revealed, will also understand the relevance of a genuine political vocation. A Christian politician can make an outstanding contribution to the welfare of the people, to the growth of culture, to social and international peace. But political activity is marked by the prophetic tradition only if these people combine great competence with absolute sincerity of motives, and display the courage to oppose dangerous tendencies, even if they seem to come from the majority. A former senator told me in private conversation that the greatest success in his political career was not to be re-elected, because he had finally made it quite clear that he was opposed to all forms of racism.

Love of neighbour and adoration of God force us, in this day and age, to be interested in political life. If we wish to make our contribution by enlightening the public, by promoting dialogue, by freeing mankind from the age-old slavery of war and terrorism, we have to renounce radically not only our individual selfishness, but also all forms of group egotism. This occasionally gives rise to suffering. However, our commitment to public life, to the economic, social, cultural and political realm requires discernment. Here again, it is of paramount importance that we find time to gather around Christ, to treasure up his word, to know him, and to be guided by his Spirit. Woe to the priests, religious and lay apostles, the Christian politicians who never know contradiction and never suffer from the hate of opposing groups. If they have the courage to live the gospel and manifest hunger and thirst for saving justice, then they also belong to Christ in his mission: '... to be a sign which men reject.... Many in Israel will stand or fall because of him, and thus the secret thoughts of many will be laid bare' (Lk 2:35). Helder Camara's coherent option for the poor has forced many people to think over and reveal their stance. Pope John was provoking violent opposition from those who were more concerned with their security and career than with the reform of the Church; this was undoubtedly one of his great sufferings.

\* \* \*

We praise you, Lord Jesus Christ. You brought to completion the history of all the prophets before you and you made your disciples alert to the fact that they have to share your suffering when they truly stand for justice and peace. Never was a human being so atrociously persecuted as you. The purity of your life and the force of your words unmasked the lies and the hypocrisy of the arrogant social classes. Even while preparing your crucifixion, they still indulged in pious talk and in the scrupulous observance of their own meticulous laws. They went so far as to insult you on the cross.

Lord, make us know your name, the name Prophet; may we honour it by all our life. Give us the strength and sincerity to listen to the discomforting prophets who awaken us from our inertia and superficiality. It is a frightening thought that we, too, could be among those who despise and persecute your prophets. Lord, preserve us from this horrifying sin. Send us your Spirit that we may truthfully believe in the Holy Spirit who has spoken and still continues to speak today through prophets.

Lord, give us the courage to live the gospel, especially when those around us try to convert us to false prudence in order to avoid all contradiction and suffering. Lord, fill us with that inner strength and joy that will enable us to bless those who curse us.

Chapter 10

# LIGHT FOR ALL THE WORLD

## 1. *Christ is the Light*

Nine times, the Lord introduces his statements by: 'Blessed'. He then turns to his disciples and gives them their mission: 'You are salt of the earth. And if the salt becomes tasteless, how is its saltness to be restored? It is now good for nothing but to be thrown away and trodden under foot. You are the light of all the world. A town that stands on a hill cannot be hidden. When a lamp is lit, it is not put under the mealtub, but on the lampstand, where it gives light to everyone in the house. And you, like the lamp, must shed light among your fellows, so that when they see the good you do, they may give praise to your Father in heaven' (Mt 5:13-16).

Here again it becomes very evident that the morality of the sermon on the mount is one with the good news. Christ in person is the gospel; he is the salt, he is the light of all the world. He gives his disciples a mission by giving them a share in his own being, in his life, in his joy, in his peace and in his light.

Christ, the eternal Word, shares with the Father the name of the One Who Is. He is the perfect visible image of the invisible God, the perfect sacrament of salvation. The Church is also called to be a sacrament, a visible sign, and we can be one to the extent only that we put our whole trust in Jesus, and give all honour to him and thus to the Father. The good news: 'You are the light of all the world' continues the mighty words at the beginning of creation: 'God said, "Let there be light", and there was light, and God saw that the light was good, and he separated light from darkness' (Gen 1:3-4). The prologue to the gospel of St John continues this great song of creation. The Word that was spoken at the beginning is itself life and light. There is nothing that has come into being by that Word that is not light. 'All that came to be was alive with his life, and that life was the light of men' (Jn 1:4). Jesus proclaims in his whole life, 'I am the light of the world'. 'No follower of mine shall wander in the dark; he shall have the light of life' (Jn 8:12). The sun is only a modest symbol of him who is the light of all the world, and he came to share with us his life and his light. 'I have come into the world as light so that no one who has faith in me should remain in darkness' (Jn 12:46).

Christ is the salt of the earth; he gives savour to everything. Without him everything is tasteless. He gives strength and clear direction to all who turn to him. As salt can give taste to the food by giving itself instead of preserving itself, so Christ gives himself totally on the cross so that all may have life, joy and peace. He has come into the world, not for his own glory, but as the splendour of the Father, who has come to illumine all those who come into the world.

The dignity and the mission of the disciples cannot be understood in any aspect unless we turn to the source of all life and light, to Christ, and put all our trust in him.

\*    \*    \*

Lord Jesus Christ, we praise you; for you are the Word of the Father. All creation manifests you as the almighty Word. We thank you for the word you spoke at the beginning: 'Let there be light'. We ask you to continue to speak this word to each and all of us: 'Let there be light'. Illumine us by sending us the Spirit of truth. We come to our own truth and find the wonderful name by which you call each person only if we acknowledge and honour you as the source of all light and life. We cannot find our way without you.

Lord, invite us, call us and urge us to follow you and to walk in your light. When your light shines upon us, then we too can be a light for others.

## 2. *You are Light*

Christ does not begin the sermon on the mount with the words 'You must' or 'you shall'. Jesus sings the most magnificent canticle of the sun: he himself being the light that makes the sun shine for all, he also illumines all people. How could he ever have said: 'You must be the light of the world' before making us aware that we receive everything — truth, grace and light from him alone? His call to us 'to let our light shine before all the world' is based on his effective word: 'You are light'; for he himself shines upon us. This, then, is the true foundation of Christian morality. In similar terms, St Paul preaches the Christian way: 'Though you were once all darkness, now as Christians you are light. Live like men who are at home in the daylight; for where light is, there all goodness springs up, all justice and truth' (Eph 5: 8-9). The apostle also makes clear to his hearers and readers that they can be light only if they awake from their selfishness and turn to Christ. 'Sleeper awake, rise from the dead, and Christ will shine upon you' (Eph 5: 14).

Whoever, in faith, receives Jesus who has come into the world to illumine all people, becomes similar to him: he is light in Christ. Therefore Paul can write to believers: 'You are children of light, children of day' (1 Thess 5: 5). Christ himself speaks of his disciples simply as 'children of the light' (Lk 16: 8), although at the same time he warns them of the danger of hiding his light; they will become fully alert and enlightened only when they are totally converted to him.

The force of Christian morality is not so much the imperative, 'Let your light shine', but the good news proclaimed by Jesus and written into our heart by the Holy Spirit: 'You are light'. Whoever accepts the good news with faith, with trust and in gratitude realizes that his mission arises from within: it is the call of grace to be truthful to one's own name, to live the new life in the light of the Lord.

Light is the symbol of purity. Jesus demands purity of heart and the intent to have our light shine out to others. There is no contradiction between the invitation to let our light shine and Jesus' words in the sermon on the mount: 'When you pray, go into a room by yourself, shut the door, and pray to your Father who is there in the secret place' (Mt 6:6). Those who want to make a show of their religion or who use religion for their own interests are no longer light and cannot turn the eyes of people to the Father in heaven. Only if we are gratefully aware of God as source of light, of life, and of all good, and thus live our morality as an ongoing thanksgiving, that is, returning all to the glory of the Father, can we truly be salt for the earth and light for the world united with Jesus Christ.

The morality of the beatitudes is, as we have seen, the morality of the paschal mystery. Jesus himself is the salt and gives savour to all things by shedding his blood on the cross, by investing all his energies in life and death in the service of his brothers. He is the light; he is not afraid to lose its splendour when he enters the darkness of Golgotha. He teaches us by his own example but even more so by his paschal mystery. 'He who cares for his own safety is lost; but if a man will let himself be lost for my sake and for the gospel, that man is safe' (Mk 8:34). 'Whoever seeks his life selfishly loses his true self; whoever gives his life for my sake finds his true self' (Mt 10:39). Christ, by surrendering himself to be crucified on the cross gives a witness of trust in the Father, and the Father glorifies him. Those who believe in the paschal mystery will be witnesses and will be ready to do everything in the name of the Lord, in the service of people; for they know that they will find their true selves, the fullness of life and light, only when they follow Jeus who came into the world to illumine all people.

\* \* \*

We thank you, Lord Jesus Christ, for giving us clear direction and mission by your word, which is a wonderful light for all; it is not just a word of your mouth; it is a word of you who are the Word of the Father. You have brought us light by the total word you have spoken by your life and your death; and the Father has sealed this word and made it glorious in your resurrection. You continue to shine upon us by sending us your Spirit. Strengthen our faith; let your light always be with us. Then we shall understand gratefully our mission to be a light for all whom we meet, and we shall grasp the many opportunities to share your gift with our fellowmen. Help us to join hands and to seek you and whatever is truthful and good together with all people of good will. Thus we shall abide in you from whom all light comes.

## 3. The social implications

The beatitudes are a great symphony, like the Canticle of the Sun, sung for the joy of all the world. Each of the beatitudes proclaimed and shared by Jesus Christ, especially the concluding verses bringing home the whole message: 'You are the light of the world', confirms Christ's radical opposition to any form of selfishness or individualism, be it in secular life or in religious life. He takes us up the mount of the beatitudes 'in view of the crowd'. He has come to be the Saviour of the world. Those who believe in him are sent to be witnesses for him, servants of their brethren, peacemakers in families, in communities, within and between nations. Jesus calls his disciples and apostles from the crowd and then sends them to the crowd for service.

Grateful acceptance of the good news and of all of God's gifts is, by its very nature, a mission to share them with others; it is a matter of God's justice that we make good use of the talents for his whole family in concern, love and service of the world in which we live. Jesus expresses this most emphatically when he adds to the good news 'You are salt of the earth' the warning: 'If salt becomes tasteless how can its saltness be restored? It is good for nothing but to be thrown away and trodden underfoot' (Mt 5 : 13). We are worth nothing if we are concerned only for ourselves. If we want to be salt for ourselves, that is, salt outside the soup, we are plainly insipid. There is no way by which savour can be restored. To be a disciple of Christ without being ready to share the joy of faith with others and become a servant of the common good is a contradiction; for how can we be salt and refuse to serve as salt, by refusing to give up our selfish self in order to bring a good savour to our *milieu*?

Again, having shared with us his light and truth, and brought forth the new creation in us ('You are the light of all the world'), Jesus points to the unbearable desire to have light only for ourselves when we receive it from him who is the Saviour and light of all the world. As long as we are true disciples of Christ, we are like a town standing on a hill; it cannot be hidden. As long as we have living faith, we are, by necessity, a living gospel; not only do we explicitly proclaim the gospel of our Lord Jesus Christ, but above all, we live the gospel in the service of our brothers and sisters, dedicated to the common good. Then can we make known him who is the origin of all that is good, that is truthful, that is beautiful.

A Christian is open to all the good in the world because he believes in the One who is the light of the world, and therefore he honours God by honouring the good whether its source be inside or outside of our Church. Unwillingness to recognize the good in others is reluctance to praise the Father in heaven. Those who do not want to use to best advantage the gifts of the one God and Father steal God's glory and honour; they waste what has been granted to them for the sake of others. Where there is living faith, there is light and there is convincing witness. However, the Lord also instructs us that we should give strict attention to our mission. We should turn our eyes as much as he does to the crowd. After having been gathered around him, and thus having found in him the source of joy and light, we shall be most anxious to share his precious gifts generously with those for whom they were given.

Pessimists waste considerable energy complaining about evil and bemoaning all that might be bad in others. Persons of living faith and trust in the Lord are not blind when they are faced with evil. However, they are light and they see first their own faults; for all good comes from God; they discover all the wonderful opportunities afforded them to serve God and their neighbour. They also help others to discover in themselves the inner resources that come from God and lead to fullness of light and life. Thus they give praise to the Father in heaven and invite all whom they meet to join them in the praise of the same Father.

* * *

Almighty God, Creator of heaven and earth, we believe that you are the almighty Father and that you can make us children worthy of you, genuine brothers and sisters who lead one another closer to you and walk in your light. We believe that you have shared all your wisdom, your might and your love with your Son, your almighty Word. By sending him to be our brother, you have given us everything. We believe in Jesus Christ, 'Light of Light', true God and true man. Through him and in him, we are sharers of your own life. And we believe that you have called us into your light by sending us your only begotten Son and the Spirit of Truth. If we entrust ourselves to you and are guided by the Holy Spirit, we shall not walk in the darkness. We are even so honoured as to become for each other a humble and healing light that turns the attention of all to you the One who is the Light of Light.

Father, we praise you for having glorified your servant, Jesus Christ, who gave his life for his brethren; you made him the source of everlasting life for all of us. We thank you for having called us to abide in Christ and thus to be salt for the earth and light for the world.

We believe in the Holy Spirit, the giver of life, who has spoken through Christ, the Prophet, and still speaks through the prophets. We trust in his gift and stand willing to fulfil our mission of being a sign of your loving presence to all in need. Help us to live our baptism and to witness to Jesus Christ who was baptized in water, in the Spirit and in his blood.

God our Father, make us firm in hope; may we now live in communion with the saints in saving solidarity, striving all together towards a new earth and a new heaven. Lord, help us to be the salt of the earth and the light of the world. Help us to serve you with a pure heart so that all who read sincerity in our service to our brethren may praise you, Father, together with the Son and the Holy Spirit, now and forever. Amen.